The Second Vatican Council has made the Christian world far more conscious of its history than it had ever been before. We cannot really understand the Council's insistence on "reform and renewal" unless we have some knowledge of how history had shaped and then perpetuated precisely those aspects of the Church's life which, in our time, cried out for new forms and new expressions for the Church's age-old mission.

For this reason, *The Unreformed Church* is an essential study for anyone who would more fully understand the Church of the twentieth century. The author, one of America's most respected Church historians, singles out four "problems" which confronted the Church at the time of the Council of Trent. These problems—the ecclesial, the liturgical, the biblical, the Christic—confronted the Church *at* Trent, but were not solved *by* Trent.

As a consequence, these unresolved problems perdured in the Church from Trent to our own day. Their unexamined presence in the life of the Church helps to explain her polemical theology, her encouragement of "devotions" rather than a liturgically centered spirituality, an almost morbid concentration on the physical aspects of Christ's Passion, with a concomitant scanting of the theological dimensions of His Resurrection, and an effective removal of the Bible from its rightful place in the center of Christian life and thought. If *aggiornamento* in the Church has been almost a trauma for many, their fearful reaction is due, in great part, to the unfortunate history of which we are all the victims as well as the heirs—the history of the unreformed Church which spans the centuries from the late Middle Ages to the Second Vatican Council.

"To be ignorant of history," observed George Santayana, "is to be condemned to repeat it." The history of the Church has never played a significant role in either the Catholic college or seminary education. That it must do so in the future is an implicit theme of this book, which, in itself, so brilliantly shows how the past—even a tragic past—can be made to serve the needs of the present.

ROBERT E. McNALLY, S.J., attended Georgetown University and Woodstock College. He received a Masters Degree from Catholic University in 1952 and a Doctorate from the University of Munich in 1957.

A former Professor of Religious Studies at George Washington University (D.C.), Father McNally is presently Professor of Church History and Liturgy at Woodstock College. He is the co-editor of *Traditio* and a frequent contributor to such magazines and journals as *America, Theological Studies, Church History* and *Medieval Studies.*

During the first-half of the 1965-1966 academic year, Father McNally served as Professor of Catholic Studies at Brown University.

The Unreformed Church *

The Unreformed Church * * *

ROBERT E. McNALLY, S.J.

SHEED AND WARD : : NEW YORK

To my students—
past, present, future—
at Woodstock College

Contents *

Contents

The Unreformed Church *

1 * Introduction

THERE IS NOTHING very startling in the fact that Christian morality was in bad need of reform in the closing days of the Middle Ages. For the Church, though constant and continuous in her inner supernatural being, is made up of human members who deviate both in faith and morals. This human element in the structure of the Church is subject to the restless ebb and flow of history, for men as products of their time live in the stream of the culture which they have created; with it they rise and fall. At the end of the Middle Ages the cultural climate of the Western world was far from conducive to high moral observance. Severe shocks on all levels of life, spiritual, intellectual and economic, had disrupted human affairs acutely and had toppled the traditional principles by which men had lived. In 1339 the devastating Hundred Years War (1339–1453) commenced between England and France; and eight years later in 1348 the dread Black Death was ravaging central Europe. The dark sense of disunity which had

seized upon Christendom was sharply underlined by the
tragedy of the Great Western Schism in the papacy, which
opened in 1378. Perhaps the definitive fall of Constantinople
to the Turks in 1453—terminating more than one thousand
years of Christian history—had a symbolic value of far greater
worth than contemporaries suspected. The general decadence,
therefore, which beset the late medieval Church simply reflected the general decadence of the late medieval world itself.

In many important respects the culture of the late Middle
Ages was ripe for a rich harvest. In almost all external forms it
had reached a high state of development, perhaps over-develop-
ment, and its total achievement merits it a significant place in
the history of culture. The middle of the fifteenth century
witnessed the invention of the printing press by Johannes
Gutenberg; at its end came the discovery of the New World by
Christopher Columbus. And these two achievements, the last
great accomplishments of the old order, are basic to the modern
world. But in a real sense medieval culture had grown until
it could grow no more. Though full, mature and ripe, it was
tired; its life in a state of desperate peril was running out. For
as fruit ripe for the harvest it was close to death. Looked at
from the point of view of the Church and her ideals, the
medieval world was virtually dead, for its heart, weighed down
with a profound pessimism, had grown cold. Gone was the
stimulating inspiration of youthful Christianity. The exaggerated preoccupation with death which is so characteristic of
this age is not surprising in view of the catastrophes in which it
was deeply involved. In fact, writes Johan Huizinga in his
classic study (in the original aptly titled, *The Autumn of the*

Middle Ages) "no other epoch has laid so much stress as the expiring Middle Ages on the thought of death."

In terms of these tremendous upheavals, which were proving at every turn so disastrous to the Christian commonwealth, it is not to be wondered that cynicism, the corrosive acid of civilization, ate its way so deep into the minds of men that the traditional discipline basic to all human conduct grew weak, and, in consequence, the standard of moral observance dipped low. What is surprising is that the Church—the papacy, the clergy and the councils—of those days seemed so utterly helpless before this almost universal decadence, religious, social and political. The state of affairs which is intimated here was not obscure. It was visible to all, clear in outline and unmistakable in significance. That the Church, which certainly had the means (more so than any other contemporary institution), did not assume active leadership in the renewal of Christian society is due ultimately neither to bad will nor to incompetence. It is more a question of that peculiarly conservative, ecclesiastical cast of mind which believes that problems, especially critical ones, somehow or other solve themselves, or can be eased by platitudes and slogans. In ecclesiastical administration there is no substitute for knowledge and courage. Lack of either or of both prepares disaster. Throughout the fourteenth and fifteenth centuries popes, emperors, saints and scholars came and went. But the *ecclesia reformanda,* more tired, more sick than ever, suffered its bitter anguish almost in silence.

To think of the Protestant Reformation of the sixteenth century as a moral crusade, directed against this general decadence so rampant in Christendom, is to misread its significance as a religious movement. For neither Martin Luther nor John Calvin considered the gross immorality which was to be seen on all levels of Christian society a cause justifying their final break with the old Church. Their principal concern was with doctrine. For in their eyes the Catholic doctrine which was preached and held by the Church of Rome did not coincide with the Christian doctrine which is contained in the Holy Scriptures. In the image of the Church ruling, teaching and sanctifying in accord with the style and practice of the Middle Ages, they could not discern to their satisfaction the resplendent figure of Christ the King, the Prophet and the Priest of whom the Holy Scriptures speak.

The reformation of the Church, because it imports a return to the biblical archetype of the Kingdom of God, must always be concerned with the Christ-image which it bears as an indelible character. No set of circumstances, no amount of violence, no display of authority can erase it. But it can be obscured from the gaze of men as indeed it was at the end of the fifteenth century. The Church of Christ, once known in Antiquity simply and reverently as 'the Mother of all the living' in parallel with the first Eve, took on in the high Middle Ages more and more the visage of a majestic, imperial queen. Law, more than life, seems to have become the significant element in the image of the Church. And this tendency, which was in accord with developments in contemporary society, manifested itself within the Church by the creation of a universal legal system which was served more and more by the faithful rather than itself serving them. The maternal aspect of the Church yielded to the regal, therefore. This was inevitable once ecclesiastical administration had become centralized under the papacy and had consolidated itself into a vast juridical bureaucracy which extended out over the whole Western world.

By the end of the Middle Ages the liturgy was in a desperate plight. Reduced to a series of peculiarly clerical, possibly even meaningless ceremonies, the laity no longer actively shared in it, because they no longer understood the meaning of these sacred rites. Divine worship was celebrated in all the churches of Christendom, and indeed with awesome splendor, but these solemnities were not ordered to inculcating in the people a distinctive liturgical piety. And yet the liturgy is by the will of Christ the ordinary means by which the Church sanctifies the faithful entrusted to her. The inspired Word of God, which had been spoken on behalf of His very own people, was relatively inaccessible. Transmitted not in the vernacular but in the venerable *Vetus latina* and the *Vulgata latina,* the Bible was for all practical purposes a closed book. Deprived of a vital, meaningful approach to divine things, the spiritual life of the faithful was not extinguished, but languished and suffered acutely from undernourishment. This suffering, neglected and underfed Church of the late Middle Ages is *the unreformed Church,* unreformed in four essential areas of her life: the ecclesial, the biblical, the liturgical and the spiritual. And it is startling to note that the authentic Catholic reform, which more than five hundred years ago was so passionately needed and prayed for, is in many respects coming to fruition only in the Johannine Council of our own day.

It is the task of Catholic reform to illuminate and clarify the fundamental assimilation of the Church to Christ the Lord. It cannot therefore be a destructive movement, for the precious *Christos-eikon* which the Church bears within her must at all costs be preserved, made brilliant and splendid before all the world. It has been rightly said that an "eikon is not an external image, foreign to its model, made from without and therefore without life in itself. An eikon is the living image of the model, through which the model is present, through which it imposes itself on the material which is to receive it." In the face of the Church as she appears at any epoch in the course of history, the inner image of Christ must be discernible. Whenever it is obscured by extraneous elements, the clarification of reform is indispensable.

There is no doubt that the conservative instinct of the Church, with the tendency to absorb and retain vestiges of all the past cultures with which she has lived, was a prime factor in the creation of *the unreformed Church*. In sifting through the traditions which have accumulated in the course of the ages, the reformer must be able to discern that authentic image according to which the Church must be restored. The reformer therefore must be a well-informed technician; he must also be in touch with the authentic Christian tradition and its constant witness to the Church through the centuries. Like every delicate work of restoration, Catholic reformation must rest on accurate knowledge. It may not proceed from chance, caprice or feeling. There must be about it an objectivity that simply transcends all personal sentiment and ephemeral practicality. The reformer must be willing to suffer deep personal pain on behalf of that Church whose good he places before his own.

But the reformation must also be motivated by the very

real consideration that the Church though founded in the far distant past lives in the present. She must be progressive without being undisciplined or uncontrolled, up-to-date without being modern or artificial, traditional without being antique or antiquated. For the timeless image of the Church, as it appears in the living Christian tradition, must constantly be put in a new setting acceptable to each succeeding generation of men. It is here especially, in the area of adaptation, that conflicting interests—the conservative and the liberal—clash over *nova et vetera,* "the new and the old," and their place in the contemporary Church. It is here, therefore, that objectivity must be re-enforced by Christian humility and charity.

Considered in its broadest aspects, the Reformation of the sixteenth century embraced a wide variety of different movements, personalities and tenets—the evangelical church of Martin Luther (Wittenberg), the extreme Anabaptism of John of Leiden (Münster), the reformed church of Ulrich Zwingli (Zürich), and the Presbyterianism of John Calvin (Geneva). Despite their individual peculiarities and theological differences, all converged in their common opposition to the traditional, historical Church, concretely to the Church of Rome at whose head stood the Pope as Christ's Vicar on earth. Each of these reforming groups (in addition to others which I have not mentioned here) believed on the basis of the Word and the Spirit of God that it had truly rediscovered in the centuries beyond the darkness of the Middle Ages *the* Church which Christ had founded; and that the Church of Rome with its pronounced papal character represented an acute aberration from the pure Gospel.

Their reform, proceeding from their new theology, centered about the doctrinal and the institutional aspects of the Church. It aimed at displacing the whole structure, both internal and external, of the old Church which historically claimed to be God's unique means of sanctification and salvation in this world. Just seventy-five years before Luther, the Council of Florence, in its decree of union (Feb. 4, 1442) for the Copts and the Ethiopians, affirmed this traditional position in the words of St. Fulgentius of Ruspe (d. 533): "No one can be saved, no matter how lavish the alms he may give, even if he should pour out his blood for the name of Christ, unless he shall remain in the bosom and unity of the Catholic Church." The Protestant rejection of this pretension was a revolution which rested on the ultimate conviction that the Church—not *any* Church but *the* Church of the Gospel—was indeed an influential instrument in the universal plan of redemption; that *the* Church, once fully restored to its evangelical purity, would assist men to holiness of life; but that the Church of Rome was not the Church of the Gospel. The movement was upward to the institution and its reformation, then downward to the individual and his reform.

The radical approach of the reformers to the difficult problems involved in ecclesiastical renovation was not totally vitiated by their break with the See of Rome. Their reform was not wholly inspired either by bad will or by bad theology. Now that the darkness of confessional passion has passed, we see today more clearly that there was in the evangelical reform movement a certain silver line of deep religious thought; and that certain of the ideas which they advanced in the area of biblical and liturgical reform have received sympathetic consideration from contemporary Catholic scholars; and in fact have even re-emerged, under Catholic auspices, in the Second Vatican Council. But these questions, however precious in themselves, touch only the periphery of the great confessional debates of the sixteenth century. They are far from the heart of the matter which concerns the very nature of the Church and its relation both to Christ and to man. For in the ultimate analysis the Church is the work of God accomplished through His redeeming Son. It is not a creation of our making.

But the powerful dialectic of reformation by pure biblical theology, comprehended apart from the living Christian tradition, led the reformers to reject the Church as an efficacious instrument for internal reformation (sanctification). The individual Christian was told to look elsewhere, to Holy Scripture and to saving faith. Salvation became the result of an I-Thou dialogue—no longer We-Thou—between God and man, a dialogue more individualistic and private than personal and ecclesial. In the eyes of the evangelical theologians of that day the Church which their reformed theology described seemed at most an external occasion, a stimulus to faith and therefore to sanctity, but certainly not the channel of all grace, the very instrument which Christ uses to carry on the work of redemption in this world.

By the middle of the sixteenth century there were clearly two different, fixed, well-defined and opposed concepts of the Church of Christ, two equally divergent concepts of salvation and the way to salvation in this world. When the dust of the fierce confessional battle had finally settled, no one was very

surprised to note that there were in the Western world two
different Christian Churches whose coexistence made the en-
durance of united Christendom impossible. The day of plural-
ism had dawned.

The Protestants were not the only reformers of the sixteenth
century. There were also groups of active Catholics who formed
part of a reform tradition which antedated the Reformation by
decades. Their proposals for the renewal of the Church were
radical and thorough, so realistic in fact, that had they been
effectively implemented it is hard to exaggerate the consequences for the subsequent history of Christendom. As Catholics devoted to the well-being of the Church as they knew
it they adopted a pattern of work which differed essentially
from that of the reformers. Ecclesial-minded to the core, they
envisioned and worked for a reform *of* the Church *by* the
Church—a reform which would indeed be conceived and
launched by private initiative but which should necessarily be
sponsored and sustained by the public authority of the Church.

It is the tragedy of the decades before the outbreak of the
Reformation that lawful authority in the Church did not
grasp the full significance of these eager voices of her "prophetic consciousness," raised on behalf of her internal renovation.
Our judgment here on ecclesiastical administration cannot be
too hard, for the competence of the Church, according to her
inner constitution and through the Divine Assistance which is
always with her, especially extends to the preservation and
cultivation of sound doctrine and pure morals. But the Church
is administered by men, at times myopic and selfish men; certainly not by angels. Her prosperity depends not only on in-

telligence but also, and to a large degree, on courage in the face of adversity. Above all it depends on the quality of her ministers' commitment to the Church herself. Because the papacy (and the Catholic episcopacy) of the fifteenth century was reluctant to pay the high price of self-reform, its successors paid the still higher price of obdurate schism in the following century. The historical lesson is striking and is still relevant.

It is one thing to boast of sound doctrine and salutary laws. It is quite another matter to live a life in conformity with this doctrine and to be saved by observing these laws. Too often the Christian, when confronted with the tragic pages of ecclesiastical history, takes refuge in the consoling thought that the Church has always held the orthodox faith and has always taught saving precepts. True! But is not the Christian challenge, courageously accepted and sincerely lived, of itself calculated to lead to an irrefutable witness to Christ, to a life, therefore, of "grace and truth"? The holiness of the Church must not be confined to the order of theory and possibility, of ways and means. Like a bright light, it must shine forth and illuminate the whole world. Sanctity, to be a true mark of the Church, must show itself more in the virtuous lives of her members than in the sacred canons of her code. It should never be forgotten that the central problem of the pre-Reformation Church was not the absence of salutary law but the failure of tepid Christians readily to observe this saving law.

To determine the exact *point de départ* of the Catholic reform is almost impossible. Its roots, deeply entangled in all phases of Catholic life, reach far back into the Middle Ages; but its most concrete expression was the Council of Trent

(1545–63) which Pope Paul III convoked to correct morals, to purify the Catholic faith and to heal the schism. The conciliar procedure which the Fathers of Trent adopted was the result of a clash of interests. It represented a compromise between the Roman curialists, who contended that the Council should deal with dogmatic questions before the reform issues, and the imperialists, who wanted the problem of reform to be central and primary. Actually the Council compromised by handling the two matters together.

The character of the first reform decree (sess. 5, June 17, 1564) is of high significance. Passed at a time when the Council was still dominated by its humanistic members, it prescribed certain definite measures for the assurance of an adequate biblical education for all priests, both regular and secular. To this end lectureships in Holy Scripture and the liberal arts (as a necessary propaedeutic) were to be established in all the dioceses and religious houses of the universal Church. This initial move towards reform foreshadowed a new, though distant, age in the Catholic Church which would be marked by a biblical-minded clergy. The conciliar debates which surrounded the formulation of this decree show that its full implications did not escape the Fathers of the Council, who saw here a clear threat to the *via antiqua,* the traditional theology of the schools. The Church History of the sixteenth and seventeenth centuries shows that this threat never became a reality, and that the clergy and the laity never became Bible-minded in the sense which the Council had hoped.

Studied in terms of the violence and peril in which the Church was involved at the time of its convocation in 1545, the

Council of Trent appears as a successful venture. As a reform synod it did bring a certain sense of stability and security to a badly shaken Church, and by its purified formulation of Catholic dogma it restored confidence to the Catholic world. In fact, the totality of its achievement was so imposing and decisive that it created its own epoch, the Tridentine Age, and gave momentum and direction to the Catholic Counter-Reformation. It deserves indeed the title, "the Iliade of our age," for its history is an epic in which great heroes contended over the momentous issue of the preservation of the Church of God.

The Council of Trent was in many respects a success, but not totally so. For it did not reconcile the dissident Protestants, and that was one of the primary reasons for its existence. In all verity, it should not be indicted either for having created the initial cause of the great separation between Catholic and Protestant, or for having denied the reformers admission to its sessions. It is more than possible that the Council of Trent, in its attitude toward the Protestants and its manner of dealing with them, was even more ecumenical minded than the current Vatican Council. But the bitter confessional spirit of the day was not conducive to a *rapprochement* which would satisfy both parties. In spite of the hostile atmosphere and the serious dogmatic issues which the Council had to face, its spirit was irenic, at least to the extent that it did not publicly condemn the Protestant reformers by name. Its pronouncements were impersonal, and in that way the door remained opened, at least slightly, for further discussion between the two factions.

The dogmatic decrees of Trent have been sharply criticized for their rigidity, for being too scholastic and too apologetic, for having erected a dividing wall between the two confessions. But the blame (if the word should be used at all) is to be placed not so much on the Fathers of Trent as on the theologians of the post-Tridentine age who saw in the Council a fixed *terminus ad quem* rather than a determined starting point for further theological investigation. And this attitude is understandable in view of the fact that in lacking historical perspective they lacked a well-defined concept of the organic development of dogma; and, further, their theology was conditioned by their felt need for defensive polemics. The acrid controversies in which they were so deeply involved required apologetes.

The Council's approach to ecclesiastical reform was dominated by the polemical atmosphere of the day. Motivated (perhaps even frightened) by the fierce attack which the Protestants had loosed on the Church, it concentrated on the reform of the individual more than of the institution. Convinced, and rightly so, that the Church as an institution of divine origin needs no reformation in her essentials, it unfortunately was too sparing in reforming her accidentals—the purely human aspects of her structure which change with the drift of history. Thus, for example, it did not extensively renovate the Roman *Curia,* the administrative structure of the Church, though this department of the ecclesiastical bureaucracy admittedly (even by the papacy itself) had been one of the chief causes of the universal scandal in Christendom. Nor did the Council attempt to suppress the Inquisition (either Roman or Spanish), which, at least, at the time must have seemed archaic and effete, certainly the prime mover of more than one *cause célèbre*. It gave no support to the great European universities and their faltering faculties of theology whose prestige continued to sink lower and lower. Far from that, it devised for the formation of priests the seminary system which, despite certain passing advantages, artificially segregated candidates for the priesthood from social life and contemporary affairs. But what most astonishes is the fact that the Council did not formulate a series of decrees defining the character and nature of the Church herself; which in the ultimate analysis was the very bone of contention and division between Catholics and Protestants.

From the vast number of problems which were then current in the days before the Council of Trent and the Catholic Reform I have selected four—the ecclesial, biblical, liturgical and spiritual—as most relevant to the theme, *the unreformed Church*. Obviously this tetrad, which has already been studied from many different points of view, deserves to be handled in a series of learned books. For this area of Church History, still relatively unexplored, is especially rich in insight into ecclesiastical life and thought. These four problems, each in its own right occupying a significant place in the cadre of Christian ideas, epitomize the historical situation of the Church on the eve of the Reformation. They represent the axis points on which the great religious upheaval of the sixteenth century turned.

Unless problems perish of their own inner insignificance, they live on. No amount of unrealistic precision lessens their cogency and force; and the fact that they grow old with the passing of time does not mean that they grow weaker. On the contrary, as they become inveterate they become stronger. The problems which this book handles were widely discussed on the eve of the Reformation and long before it. They were known to everyone who was *au courant* with the movement of contemporary ideas. The reformers made issue of them and offered their own solutions which varied in degrees of radicalism. But the Council of Trent despite its achievements in other areas presented almost nothing in the way of a solution to these four problems.

In our own day, after more than four hundred years of uncertainty and hesitation, the Catholic Church assembled in the Second Vatican Council has turned to a serious examination of her own structure, of her relation to the Word of God and the Sacrament of Christ, of their place in the spiritual life of her faithful, of her commitment to the contemporary world. In terms of historical consideration it is striking to note that the problems which most engage our attention today were born centuries before the discovery of the American continent. That the modern Church has undertaken the solution of these medieval problems is a vivid sign of their perennial universal character.

We live in an age that has been characterized by ecumenism as an attempt to transform four hundred years of Catholic-Protestant coexistence into more intelligent, charitable, meaningful cohabitation in this world. The goal is attainable, but not without mutual understanding. And here the Catholic, sensitive because for him Protestantism represents schism, must study the exact circumstances, motivation and method under which this great division of Christendom took place. Examined in the light of both historical and contemporary events, the schism of the sixteenth century must inspire humility in the hearts of both Catholics and Protestants who are concerned for the oneness of the Lord's flock and fold in this world.

The purpose of this book is modest. Without prejudice to other aspects of the whole problematic, it seeks to present a synthesis of one phase of *the unreformed Church,* to focus attention clearly, I hope, back through the pages of Church History to a series of questions which were once posed but never answered. I have not attempted more than to sketch the theme in broad outline and to emphasize relevant conclusions. I have not tried to say all that could be said. But I trust that what I have written here is sufficient to delineate the general picture of *the unreformed Church.* Frequent references are given in the footnotes for those who wish to pursue the dialogue of the text further. A selected bibliography is added for those who have been persuaded that the theme of the book is worth further study. I have inserted a chronological table to assist the reader through the intricate web of events which enter into this book, and an index to assist him in controlling the text.

One last word here. Because I believe that the historian is essentially a pedagogue—like the instructed Scribe "who brings forth from his storeroom things new and old"—I have not hesitated in these pages to use history to instruct my readers about the past and the present. "History maketh a young man to be old," wrote Thomas Fuller, "without either wrinkles or gray hairs; privileging him with the experience of age without either the infirmities or inconveniences thereof." It is with this adage in mind that I have put this book together.

2 * Church

THE PRIMITIVE CHURCH THOUGHT of herself in biblical terms. She was the people of God, the Body of Christ, the Lord's flock, His Spouse, the branches whose vine was Christ. In the first centuries after the close of the apostolic age the Christian consciousness of its close alliance with God and its special role in His universal plan of redemption is in clear evidence. As a believing and worshipping community the unity of the faithful in creed, code and cult was of the highest importance, for it was rooted in the oneness of Word and Sacrament; and it expressed the Church's special ethos as God's unique Kingdom of the last days. The Christians of the first generation were deeply impressed with their vocation to witness Christ to the world about them by word and deed, but especially by blood and life. To be a witness was to be a martyr; and to be a martyr was to testify to Christ by the totality of life itself. This heroic act, inspired by charity, was the Church's ultimate answer to the demands of the Roman empire. Her definitive negation of Caesar's outrageous claim to be Lord (*Kurios*) earned her the scorn of the contemporary world; but it also earned her in the end a decisive victory over the whole empire of Caesar.[1]

The primitive Christians were ecclesial minded. Their relation to their Church was expressed in vital terms. She was "the true mother of all the living" who begat them into eternal life.[2] She was "the new Eve" who stood at the head of the new creation which her Spouse, Christ the Lord, "the new Adam," had wrought. St. John Chrysostom (d. 407) expressed it this way:[3]

For just as Eve was produced from the side of Adam, so too we from the side of Christ . . . But that the Church took shape from the side of Christ, where could we find proof of this? This too Scripture reveals. For after Christ was lifted up on the Cross . . . one of the soldiers came nigh and pierced His side . . . From that blood and water the whole Church has its being and existence . . . Just as the woman was fashioned from Adam in sleep, so the Church was formed from the side of Christ in death.

The significance of the relation of Adam to Eve which the saint discovers in Scripture brings out clearly in terms of salvation history the vital relation of Christ to His Church.

Through the Church men died mystically with Christ, to rise with Him in the glory of a new life; through the Church, too, they passed unharmed through the waters of the Red Sea, purified and united to God's people en route to the heavenly Jerusalem. In the wilderness of this life a new manna descended from heaven to sustain, buoy up and refresh their weariness. This new bread of life was at once testimonial to the saving death of Christ and bond of charity cementing the faithful to one another. In the vocabulary of the early Christians, words such as mother, birth, life, are prominent. These terms described the vitality of their mystical relation to the Church. It is significant that one of the earliest acts of the martyrs epitomizes the complexity of Christian ideas in the phrase, "the mystery of simplicity."[4]

Face to face with the decaying world which surrounded him, the Christian felt that he had a significant contribution to make to contemporary society. Thus an unknown writer of the third century, in a remark foreshadowing the Church's role in the development of culture, observes: "What the soul is in the body, that the Christians are in the world."[5] That is, they are the principle of life, unity, love and reason. Through their presence in the world, the whole cosmic composite is seen as taking on new meaning and significance. In retrospect the role of the Church in the ancient world appears vital in the sense that all true evolution is an expression of life. It did not merely preserve what it found. Rather it transformed the old civilization, without however standing outside the process. It operated in close affiliation with society. But the Church, "this new blood and spirit," was itself influenced by the very world which it was transforming.[6]

The early Christian communities, for example Rome, Alexandria and Antioch, were essentially assemblies of the faithful gathered about and under their bishops who stood in the place of the Lord. St. Ignatius of Antioch (*ca.* 110) in his *Epistle to the Ephesians* describes the relation in these words:[7]

Surely, Jesus Christ, our inseparable life, for His part is the mind of the Father, just as the bishops, though appointed throughout the vast, wide earth, represent for their part the mind of Jesus Christ.

The orthodoxy of the apostolic witness to the Risen Lord was proved and certified by the state of peace and harmony which subsisted between all the believing communities of the world. Those who could not, or would not, hear the voice of the Good Shepherd echoing in the Church were clearly not of His flock and were cast out.[8]

Christ presided over the universal Church. His constant protection and guidance were reflected in the persons of the bishops who presided over particular churches. "How much more do I count you happy," wrote St. Ignatius to the Ephesians, "who are so closely knit to him (the bishop) as the Church is to Jesus Christ, and as Jesus Christ is to the Father."[9] As successors of the Apostles they were the custodians of the faith, the priests *par excellence,* the representatives of Christ to His people. The first believers, who turned to St. Peter and his companions with the words, "Brethren, what shall we do?" (Acts 2:37) established a pattern for the relation of the people to their bishop. For he was *the* teacher of Christian doctrine.

Seated on a simple *cathedra* rather than on a regal throne, the bishop exercised his magisterial office. The people, gathered before him, gratefully accepted the proclaimed Word of God as a new food from heaven. It nourished their faith as the Sacrament of Christ sustained their charity. In a series of biblical commentaries which have survived from Christian antiquity the voices of these venerable bishops can be heard once again as they open up for their people the richness of the evangelical kerygma which they had received. What stands out clearly in the sources of ancient Church History is the bishop's conscientious execution of his magisterial office, the preaching of the Gospel and the teaching of the people. In proportion as this evangelical ideal was lost the Church decayed.[10]

The Catholic bishop was protector of the poor, the widow and the orphan; he was patron of the prisoner of war, the slave and the unfortunate; and he was provider for the hungry, sick and destitute. His sociological role was so decisive for civilization that in the course of the years after the collapse of the Roman administration in northern Europe—the barbarian period—the whole burden of law and order was thrust on him. This is understandable not only in view of the sacred character of his office and the deep confidence which the people put in him, but also in terms of the ancient Roman tradition of law and order which he represented. In these dark hours of crisis the Catholic episcopacy did not shrink from personal involvement in the problems of society to whose restoration and preservation it was committed. More often than not the expectations of clergy and laity were realized in the accomplishments of the man whom they had freely elected their bishop.[11]

The primitive Church was not pneumatic and spiritual in the sense that it was without law and organization. Both elements were present, and both centered in the bishop, though the juridical structure of the Church at this time was essentially simple, functional and free from the legal complexity which characterizes the medieval Church. The Church was not centralized in her juridical aspects; nor was there any single, positive legal code for the universal Church. Normally the bishop with his *presbyterium,* the principal clergy of his see, or with other bishops in synod, handled the difficult problems of faith and morals which touched the spiritual well-being of their dioceses. The orientation was pastoral (Word and Sacrament) and charitable (spiritual and corporal works of mercy).

But the early Church was not a communion of saints. It was not an ideal, golden age. As early as the middle of the first century (*ca.* 57) St. Paul found it necessary to rebuke the scandalous Christians of Corinth in these words (1 Cor. 11: 18–22):

I hear that when you meet in church there are divisions among you . . . So then when you meet together, it is no longer possible to eat the Lord's Supper. For at the meal each one takes first his own supper, and another drinks overmuch. Have you not houses for your eating and drinking? Or do you despise the Church of God?

And in the persecution of the Christians by the emperor Decius (d. 251), the church of Carthage witnessed a mass apostasy from the faith. St. Cyprian (d. 258), in his work, *De lapsis,* was at pains to trace this wholesale defection of his faithful from Christ to a lack both of "mercy in works" and "discipline in morals."[12] A century later the Church both in the East and West was torn almost to shreds by the scandal of the Arian heresy. Other confirmatory examples of equal pertinence can be cited. The picture, therefore, of Christian life in the early Church is neither simply black nor white. It has its bright and dark moments, but in no sense is it without blemish. But the spiritual ideals and the mode of expressing them which we discover in the Church of these early centuries offer valuable insight into the evangelical spirit of primitive Christianity.

The greatest external problem of the ancient Church was her relation to Empire, Caesar and culture. From her initial confrontation with these three factors she emerged as the Church of the Martyrs (*ca.* 64–313), the Christian community silently suffering at the hands of a world which did not understand her.[13] These first centuries produced no political theories of Church and State. The approach was more direct and simple. Surrounded by the mighty power of the empire, the Church held on to the wisdom of her Saviour (Mt. 22:21): "Render to Caesar the things that are Caesar's, and to God the things that are God's," and in terms of this evangelical dichotomy she expressed her own aspirations for liberty. The Fathers were even willing to pray for the persecuting Caesars; and in the majestic law and order of the empire they saw that beneficial force which was holding back the advance of the anti-Christ into this world.[14]

Until 313 the Church was illicit in the Roman Empire. She was outlawed and *non grata*. But in the three centuries since her foundation she had become a world power with which Caesar, in the person of the emperor Constantine (d. 337), had to reckon. Legal persecution had proven ineffectual in retarding her progressive growth; nor had religious syncretism been able to absorb her. Thus the imperial decision of Constantine in 313 to give legal recognition to the Church was realistic. Without becoming in point of law the imperial religion, the

Church was granted an accredited position within the legal framework of the empire. Through the liberality of the emperor she enjoyed privileges and benefits in recognition of her *de facto* importance in the Roman World. Naturally this "half Christian" emperor expected the Church to be useful to the empire, to secure for it that imperial unity of which Diocletian had dreamed when he reorganized the Roman constitution.[15]

Constantine's legal recognition of the Church seemed to assure her freedom; but the new responsibilities which this concession entailed subjected her to the old empire in new ways. Up to the first decade of the fourth century the Roman emperors represented pagan hostility. But with the coming of the sons of Constantine to the throne the imperial family had become Christian, and the Church experienced the first serious attempts of the empire to absorb her into the civil service. By the middle of the century, the passionately Arian Constantius II (337–361), ruthless emperor and amateur theologian, was demonstrating the misery which the Church would inevitably reap as one of the first fruits of an unhealthy affiliation with *Imperium*. For this pagan sovereign (baptized later on his death-bed) for interests of his own presumed to revise the Catholic faith along Arian terms and to impose this alien theology on the Church with a ruthlessness which was unheard of up to that time.[16] That the Church did not succumb to the official Arianism of the emperor is a sign of that moral miracle which ultimately is an expression of her divine origin.

In 380 by imperial decree of Theodosius the Great (d. 395)[17] the Catholic Church became the official religion of the empire. "It is our pleasure," wrote the emperor, "that all the nations, which are governed by our Clemency and Moderation, should steadfastly adhere to the religion which was taught by St. Peter to the Romans; which faithful tradition has preserved; and which is now professed by the Pontiff Damasus and by Peter, Bishop of Alexandria. . . ." To be a Roman, therefore, was to be a Catholic; and to be a Catholic was to profess 'the faith of the Apostle Peter,' transmitted by Rome (West) and Alexandria (East). Gradually the law of the Church coalesced with the law of the empire so that the religious and political foundation of the *Respublica Christiana* was laid.[18] The introduction to a new volume in the history of the Church was being prepared.

In the East where she found a developed cultural and political pattern, including Caesaro-papism, the Church had no choice but to conform. In the West, however, she was freer, more active and decisive in the creation of the new medieval civilization, for here she was able to work in an atmosphere less determined by historical presuppositions and more receptive to her leadership. Here, too, at an early date the moral prestige of the Christian Church comes into evidence. In the distinguished person of St. Ambrose (d. 397) of Milan, who found in an ecclesiastical career the vocation to historical greatness, the Church found a worthy spokesman for her ideals.[19] His dramatic castigation (including a salutary punishment) and humiliation of Emperor Theodosius for the massacre of Thessalonica (390) established the Church as the supreme moral force in the Western world.

That the early Church made no pretense to absorb the temporal authority of the empire by her claim to moral supremacy in this world is attested by the celebrated letter of Pope Gelasius I (d. 496) to the eastern emperor Anastasius I.[20] Here the pope describes *Imperium* and *Sacerdotium* as two authorities "by which this world is chiefly (*principaliter*) ruled: the sacred authority of the popes and the royal power." Both are rooted in the same God as their ultimate source; both are independent and adequate. But the royal authority, which is supreme, is not absolute. For the temporal sword which it holds in its hands as an instrument of peace and security is ordered to the service of the temporal and spiritual interests of the Church. The emperor as defender of Christendom, of which the Christian Church is both firm pillar and foundation-stone, is obliged to heed her appeal in crisis; he is also obliged to heed her moral counsel, because the Church must render an account to God for his soul. The pure Gelasian formula, however, lapsed into unfortunate obscurity in the face of new developments which were carrying the Church in new directions. When revived, the ambiguity of the text allowed itself to be twisted to the favor both of the imperialists and the curialists.

The integrity and supremacy of the Roman Empire were shattered by the fifth- and sixth-century invasions of the Franks and Goths. These new peoples were the raw material from which the medieval world was to be formed. These barbaric, uncultured non-Christians (or Semi-Arians) contained within themselves the seeds of a brilliant, productive culture which would prevail in the West for more than one thousand years. But no one in the year 500 could have suspected that. What is of special importance to the history of the Church in this regard is that the Frankish nation (occupying northern France and

parts of north-western Germany) had by the middle of the
eighth century reached a moment when it was already on the
path to historical greatness.

After almost three centuries the old Merovingian House—
the dynasty of 'the do nothing kings'—had become virtually
effete. The ancient order was passing, in fact tottering under
burdens which its own official lethargy was incapable of bearing. In the ambitious family of Pepin a new ascendancy had
been born, and herein the Frankish kingdom was to find its
destiny to supremacy in the Western World. But the legitimate
transference of the royal crown from the decadent Merovingian
Childerich III to the powerful Carolingian Pepin III (d. 768)
could not be justified on the basis of hereditary right, the Germanic *Blutrecht,* which the new claimant obviously lacked. It
was under these circumstances that the celebrated question was
posed in 749 to Pope Zachary I (d. 752). Asked by the legates
of Pepin who should rule the Frankish kingdom, the pope replied: "It would be better that that man be called king who
has the power rather than that man who is without royal
power."[21] In these words the papacy nodded assent to the transference of kingship from Childerich, the *de iure* king, to Pepin
who *de facto* was exercising authority in the Frankish kingdom.

This was indeed a decisive moment in papal history. For
here the papacy's moral prestige in the universal Church was
sought and accepted as a substitute for *Blutrecht* in establish-
ing a new dynasty. It shows the position of majesty which the
Roman pontiff occupied in the eyes of the Franks. For, in
supporting the candidacy of Pepin, it entered deeply (more
deeply than it suspected) into the formation of medieval civi-

lization in the West; and significantly, at the very time that the papacy was sealing this new Frankish-Roman union, the old alliance between Rome and Byzantium which had united pope and emperor since the days of Constantine was dissolving. This new politic of the papacy was further confirmed and strengthened by St. Boniface (d. 754), the Anglo-Saxon Apostle of Germany, a missionary whose Christianizing of the Germanic people was ordered to uniting them directly to the Holy See.[22] Imperceptibly the loose strings which had united Western Christendom under the papacy were being drawn tighter.

The new alliance of the Church of Rome with the Frankish kingdom imported drastic transformations in the character of both. In 752 Boniface with holy oil anointed Pepin, who had been elected king the year before by the magnates of the kingdom assembled at Soissons.[23] Later, in 754, Pope Stephen II crossed the Alps to visit personally the new Frankish king and to discuss with him the character of the relationship which should be established between them. The results of this historic meeting were far-reaching. At the royal abbey of St. Denis the pope anointed the king, and the king in turn at Quierzy conferred on the pope sovereignty over that principality known as the Patrimony of St. Peter. The papal unction drew the Frankish king into the ecclesiastical orbit, while the royal donation constituted the pope a temporal sovereign. But more than that, King Pepin freely obligated himself to be the protector of the Church of Rome, and the pope freely accepted this royal patronage. For the moment this arrangement—the influence of the Roman Pontiff in Germany and of the Frankish king in Italy—satisfied the interests of both.

With the coming of Pepin's son Charles the Great to the Frankish throne in 768, all was ready for the final stage of this dramatic development. On Christmas Day 800 Pope Leo III placed the imperial crown on Charles' head in the venerable Constantinian basilica of St. Peter which joyously echoed and re-echoed with the acclamations of clergy and people. The light of the new day which had dawned fell on the new *Sacrum Imperium* of the West with which the papacy would now stand as it had formerly stood with the Byzantine empire. The unprecedented act of Pope Leo would influence Western history for more than one thousand years.[24]

The coronation of the Frankish king (*rex Germanorum et Langobardorum*) by the pope as active agent signified that the imperial title depended on the Holy See; that this new Frank-ish-Germanic empire had its roots deep in the historical past (*translatio imperii*), in old Byzantium and in the Roman Em-pire; and that the emperor's office in its spiritual aspects im-ported the temporal obligation (*patrocinium*) of defending the Pope, the Church and Christendom. Thus were born new rela-tions between *Italia* and *Germania,* between *Imperium* and *Sacerdotium,* which are the warp and woof of medieval Church History. But the full meaning of these new relations would become apparent only in the fury of the centuries ahead.

The political-ecclesiastical problems of the Middle Ages cen-tered not in Church-State (as two distinct, independent, op-posed entities) but in Christian society (as a political, cultural, religious unity), over which two heads, spiritual and temporal, pope and emperor, presided. Because the medieval emphasis invariably falls on the aspect of unity rather than diversity,

the *Respublica Christiana,* Christendom, was seen as founded
in the oneness of Christ represented by one pope and one
emperor. The concern was more with Christian society than
with the Christian state; but the lines distinguishing Christian
society and Christian state crossed and blended at many points.
The moment of convergence, the so-called middle zone, the
area of mixed interests both spiritual and temporal, was the
center of conflict between *Imperium* and *Sacerdotium* (as it
is between Church and State). And this fine point was too
often obscure.

A letter which Charles sent to Pope Leo III in 796 points
up the inclination to control the Church which will mark the
relations of the medieval German monarchs with the Holy
See:[25]

It is our part with the help of divine holiness to defend by armed
strength the holy Church of Christ everywhere from the outward
onslaught of the pagans and the ravages of the infidels, and to
strengthen within it the knowledge of the Catholic Faith. It is your
part, most holy Father, to help our armies with your hands lifted up
to God like Moses, so that by your intercession . . . the Christian
people may . . . have victory. . . .

The pope's place is 'in the sacristy,' with hands uplifted in
prayer; the emperor's is on the battlefield, with drawn sword.
The emperor's role is temporal, the pope's spiritual. But the
words, "to strengthen within it the knowledge of the Catholic
Faith," give the emperor a special portal through which to enter
the spiritual realm. They open the door, however slightly, to

Caesaro-papism. But within two centuries the papacy would have slammed it shut.

With the death of Ludwig das Kind in 911, the celebrated Carolingian dynasty died out. Deprived of its great protector to the North, the papacy in Rome declined sharply. Prey to many destructive forces, but especially to the decadent, ambitious Roman nobility, it experienced the darkest hours in all its history. And the fury of Islam which threatened the West served to make the already heavy burden of the papacy even more intolerable.

During the Frankish period *Imperium* protected and guided the Holy See; under the Saxon kings (919–1024) it domineered and mastered the Church. Otto I (926–973), the restorer of the ancient *Imperium Romanum,* laid the foundation of a powerful Germanic empire on the basis of a politico-ecclesiastical synergism: the *Reichsbischöfe,* bishops who at one and the same time played a double role, spiritual (in the Church) and temporal (in the Empire). These prince-bishops belonged to the emperor. For from his hands they had received both the spiritual and temporal insignia of their office.[26] In virtue of their princely state they shared in the temporal administration; but in virtue of their sacerdotal state these celibates could not transmit their temporal holdings and titles to their progeny. Thus, by a clever administrative and financial arrangement the emperor enjoyed the support of a strong moral and political force—the most educated and capable churchmen of the realm—without, however, any consequent continuing obligation on the part of the empire. It constituted the Ottonian *Reichskirche*—the so-called imperial church—which encompassed within the cadre of its centralized feudalism every bishop and abbot of the empire. In effect it made the Germanic episcopacy more dependent on the emperor than on the pope.

In Rome on February 2, 962 Otto I ('the Great') was crowned emperor by Pope John XII (955–964).[27] In the *Pactum Ottonianum,* which he concluded with the pope on February 13th, the traditional privileges of the Holy See were confirmed, the emperor's responsibilities toward it acknowledged, and the imperial rights over papal elections reaffirmed in accord with the *Constitution* of Lothar of 824. What is clearly set forth in this document is Otto's supremacy over Rome. When, therefore, Pope John dared to rebel against the imperial authority, he was, in accord with the principles of the *Reichskirche,* deposed (Dec. 4, 963) by a Roman synod; and Leo VIII, a layman, was elected pope and consecrated with the 'new' liturgy which the emperor had introduced into Italy. What the emperor could do with the bishops in Germany, he now presumed to do with the pope in Rome. After Otto's departure from the city, Pope John returned from exile and secured from a Roman synod the deposition of his rival, Leo. But on the sudden death of John the Romans elected Benedict V ('the Grammarian'), who in turn was deposed and banished, while Leo continued as pope until his death. The papacy was now indeed reaping the fruits of its close affiliation with *Imperium.*

In the course of these violent proceedings the relations between *Sacerdotium* and *Imperium* underwent serious revision. The concept of papal protection in the Gelasian sense (the emperor as 'arm of the Church') changed into the concept of imperial protection in the Teutonic-royal sense (the emperor as supreme *patronus*). Previously the popes had notified the Germanic emperors of the fact of their election in order that the Church might at once be assured of the imperial protection. Now, in accord with Otto's new conception, the Romans were forced to take an oath not to elect a pope without the emperor's consent, while the pope-elect was to swear in the presence of imperial legates that before his consecration he would inform the emperor of his election and await his confirmation. The extension of the concept of the *Reichskirchentum* to the See of Rome could only result in the gradual absorption of the pope as bishop of Rome into the orbit of the imperial Church of Germany. And thus gradually the universal Church, deprived of its autonomy, would wither and die.

Emperor Otto I had control of the papacy and he used his power in papal affairs. On the death of Leo VIII in 965 the Romans sent a delegation to him in Saxony to ask whom he wished as pope. He nominated John, nobleman of the House of Theophylactus and bishop of Narni, whom the Romans obediently elected as John XIII (965–972). How extreme and absolute the imperial protection of the Holy See became the Salian emperor Henry III (1039–1056) demonstrated at the synod of Sutri in 1046. Here this *unctus Domini* and *vicarius Christi* in whom the sacral-priestly character of the Christian monarch is so strikingly expressed, deposed three 'popes,' Gregory VI, Sylvester III and Benedict IX, and set up a German as Pope Clement II (1046–47), who, while bishop of Rome, continued to be bishop of Bamberg.

It was inevitable that sooner or later the Christian Church would react against her progressive secularization.[28] This happened in the second half of the eleventh century. Born of the evangelical conviction that the spiritual is superior to the temporal, the reform movement centered about the freedom of the Church in this world. For the reformers this was God's Will and they adhered to it stubbornly. In formulating their program they found inspiration in the ideals of Cluny, its other-worldly spirit, its centralization, its purity of faith and morals. The reform movement enjoyed the sympathy and co-operation of a group of competent, scholarly, energetic church-men who in the general decadence of ecclesiastical life saw an acute need for renovation. The revision of the constitutional character of the Church, as it then was, formed the pivot around which their reform activity turned.

The reform of the eleventh century ultimately achieved the liberation of the Church from secular bondage. But this achievement, which had effectively subtracted her from the orbit of the empire, placed her directly under the authority of the papacy which then found itself presiding over a cen-tralized Church. Thereby was born a whole series of new crises, conflicts and serious internal problems which remain to this day. For this was central to the architecture of the medieval Church, that the Catholic bishops be preserved from rigid, exaggerated centralization under either *Imperium* or *Sacer-dotium,* that they freely subsist in a middle zone of simultane-ous freedom from and obligation to the two, since they were subjects of both pope and emperor.

The first great movement of the Church upward from the feudalistic bondage of the Germanic emperors was the work of Nicholas II (1058–61). It was the double good fortune of this pope to have succeeded the reform popes, Victor II (1055–57) and Stephen IX (1057–58), and to have been elected to the papacy during the minority of the German king Henry IV (1056–1106) who, as a child, was powerless to resist the constitutional revolution which the pope was preparing. By the papal decree of April 1059, *In nomine Domini,* "the constitution of the Church in the future" was provided for in a way that would inevitably lead to strife between Pope and emperor.[29] Henceforth, the cardinal-bishops were to be the unique and sole electors of the pope. The cardinal-clerics, the lower clergy and the people of Rome were permitted the right of consent and acclamation, while the participation of the German emperor was politely ("saving due honor and reverence for our beloved son, Henry . . .") but effectively excluded from this important function in the internal administration of the Church.

This courageous and far-sighted act of Pope Nicholas was ultimately to prove of the highest value in the liberation of the papacy from lay control. The pope would no longer serve Christendom as a *Reichsbischof,* an imperial chaplain whom the emperor could as easily annihilate as create. The fact that this pope had worn at his coronation a dual crown (spiritual and temporal) was an ominous sign of the future.[30] Freed from the control of the emperor, the papacy passed more and more into the possession of the Roman cardinals whose rise to power took its point of departure from Nicholas' revision of the papal election law.

In the person of Hildebrand, Gregory VII (1073–85), the Church received a leader capable and desirous of reforming it. Energetic, experienced, religious and fearless, he was inspired by two key ideas: 'the freedom of the Church' and 'the justice of God.' For him these notions were not abstractions, but the foundation of his reform program. The liberty of the Church meant "freedom from secular duties and the influence of the state, but also freedom of the Church to carry out its mission, the conversion of the world—and this last necessarily involves the leadership of the world."[31] His understanding of justice was derived from the consideration that this freedom— "the freedom of Christ"—was guaranteed by God's authority and must be respected as a right. In this world the right order of things, the order of freedom and justice, would establish a reign of peace.[32] To formulate and implement this program, even to the point of dismantling the ecclesiastical-political constitution of the empire, was Gregory's vocation.

But the freedom which Gregory envisioned for his bishops was a freedom neither of license nor of autonomy. In his vision of the Church, which his successors in the course of the following century were to realize, the only valid position of the Catholic bishops was union with and dependence upon the bishop of Rome, Christ's vicar.[33] From personal experience Gregory knew well the evils which the deformed relation between papacy and episcopacy had wrought among the bishops.[34] His reform therefore was aimed at restoring a just balance between the two. In the *Dictatus papae,* a list of twenty-seven propositions on the papacy, Gregory enunciated his lofty conception of the pope's position in Christendom:[35]

> That the Roman Pontiff can depose or re-
> instate bishops.
> That he may depose emperors.
> That he himself may be judged by no one.
> That the Roman Church has never erred,
> nor ever, by the witness of Scripture,
> shall err in all eternity.

As occasion demanded Gregory implemented the teaching of
the *Dictatus papae*. The result was both a revolution and a
reformation.

The *Registrum*[36] of Pope Gregory shows that his authority
and influence extended by letter and legate over the most distant parts of the universal Church. His concern was principally
with the episcopacy. He freely named bishops, transferred and
deposed them, dictated advice to them and gave reprimand and
praise. During his pontificate began the practice whereby
metropolitans under whom their own suffragans were hier-
archically ordered, took an oath of fidelity to the pope, to defend the papacy and to heed its counsels. At the same time the
pallium became more and more a sign of special adherence to
and communion with the Holy See. This Romeward motion
of the episcopacy spiraled upward to the pope, who occupied
the pinnacle of a closely centralized feudal society. Progressively the Church became a strong fortress of power, but one
isolated mentally from the surrounding world whose spirit she
found pronouncedly uncongenial.[37]

But the politic of Gregory was not motivated by lust of power
for its own sake or for self-glorification.[38] This pope made no
sinister pretense to substitute *Sacerdotium* for *Imperium*. The
centralization of the Church for which he was responsible
was an historic corollary to the decentralization of the Germanic *Reichskirche,* which he opposed on principle as an
aberration from the mind of Christ. In his conception of the
right order of things which should prevail in Christendom, the
Church was not a department of the empire, nor a body with
two visible heads, pope and emperor. Rather it was a sacred

society presided over by Christ in the person of His Vicar, a flock to be segregated and protected from unclean civil authority,[39] ecclesiastical simony and clerical concubinage. If the ultimate accomplishment of the Lord's designs required a centralized Church, an episcopate obedient to the pope alone, a purified and reformed clergy, Gregory was willing and eager to be the author and promotor of the program which would give birth to this renewal. If the empire must die that the Church might live, that too was acceptable to his reform thinking.

The history of the celebrated struggle between the German king Henry IV and Pope Gregory VII over their respective rights *in* and *over* Christendom is epical. The excommunication of the king, his public penance on the snowy summit of Canossa, the imperial counter-thrust against the pope in Rome, and his abject death in exile[40] are among the most stirring episodes in the history of the Church. The struggle between *Imperium* and *Sacerdotium* was a contest to the end over the principle—clear in theory but obscure in practice—that the pope as Christ's Vicar heads the Church on earth. The decisive question posed at that time concerned the Church. What concretely is she? For by reason of the close penetration and conpenetration of the sacerdotal and imperial elements, well-defined spheres of right and influence were not easily distinguished in Christian society. In the context of medieval civilization the two powers seemed to blend almost perfectly; in consequence the struggle to distinguish and separate was most bitter. The theological question of the headship of the Church was inevitably translated into the complex, delicate question of the headship of Christendom which *de facto* embraced the whole Western World.

The Investiture Controversy was officially terminated by the Concordat of Worms (1122) concluded between Pope Callixtus II (1119-24) and Emperor Henry V. The cause had been a just one; the war violent but inevitable; the victory questionable. Despite various legal concessions and clauses of honor which were made to the emperor, the Gregorian principles ultimately prevailed. The pope became in fact, as he was in law, the sole visible head of the Church, its *caput et cardo*. Under him directly and immediately stood the Catholic episcopacy which the papacy had saved from the cold grave of secularization. When in the course of the years the results of the contest were harvested, sifted and evaluated, its full meaning became clear. The universal episcopacy was centralized under the pope in such a constitutional relationship as the Church had never before experienced; and the cardinals had been gradually exalted into an oligarchic position of first importance in the administration of the Church. By the late Middle Ages the Church had become a closely structured monarchy presided over by the Holy See which was now understood in a special sense as an administrative aristocracy composed of the pope together with the cardinals.[41]

When Nicholas II in 1059 revised the papal election law, it was most reasonable to entrust the election of the pope to the cardinal-bishops. They represented the principal clergymen of the pope's diocese, were active in their support of the Roman concept of the Church, and loyal to the Holy See. But at first the papacy did not fully comprehend the true character of this revolutionary legal maneuver which it had contrived as a saving constitutional reform. For in the cardinalate—a *collegium,* founded neither in divine revelation nor in canonical tradition—a new aristocracy had been created. It would develop as an oligarchy of power which at times would moderate, at times tyrannize, over the autocracy of the papacy.

With the reformation of the Church in the eleventh century the cardinalate took shape as a permanent administrative *collegium.* The functional change was considerable, for up to this time the office of the cardinals had been essentially liturgical— to care for and to preside over worship in the principal churches (*tituli*) of Rome. Now the college became an official executive organ; new offices of trust in the Church were held by cardinals in virtue of the very fact that they were cardinals; and significantly the ancient legal term *Curia* is first used at this time (1089) to designate this *collegium,* the collectivity of the cardinals, as special advisors of their head, the pope.[42]

Thus the character of the cardinalate changed drastically as the old *palatium Lateranense* was gradually reshaped into the *Curia Romana* comprising the totality of the papal court. Whereas at an earlier date the pope had been assisted in the government of the Church of Rome by the *presbyterium* of his diocese (and, at times, by other bishops in synod), now he came to rely more and more on the college of cardinals. As the authority of the Holy See became more centralized and universal, the role of the cardinals in the Church became more prestigious. They became, as St. Peter Damiani wrote, the *spirituales ecclesiae universalis senatores*—the Senators of the Church universal.[43] The development here runs in the direction of a unified world Church, subject to a common law, worshipping in the same rite, and administered by the pope with the cooperation of his cardinals *in Curia.*

Two contemporary documents from the early curial circle are instructive for the insight they offer into the influences operative in the formation of the *Curia.* In a work intended for the curial cardinals, St. Peter Damiani, under the influence of imperial *Renovatio,* holds up the Roman *senatus* for their consideration. "The Roman Church," he writes, "must imitate the ancient *Curia* of the Romans." As the old senate once reduced all nations to obedience to the Roman empire, so the cardinals, the custodians of the apostolic see, must strive "that the human race be subject to the laws of Christ, the true emperor."[44] In another document (1089), addressed to the citizens of Velletri by Pope Urban II (1088–99), their relation to the *Curia* is set forth in terms of Germanic feudalism.[45] Thus two streams of influence—Roman, the senate-idea, and Germanic, the feudal idea—enter into the concept of the *Curia* as it developed historically.

The chief administrative vehicle of this *Curia* was the so-called *consistorium,* the plenary gathering of the cardinals under the pope for the purpose of discussing and deciding all important ecclesiastical matters (*causae maiores*), for example questions of dogma, finance, justice and the like. And these matters were generally of universal interest. The consistory, for example, was consulted on issues such as the condemnation of *Magna Carta* (1215), the Throne Controversy (1197–1212) in the empire, the excommunication of Emperor Frederick II in 1227, and similar matters of international import, whether spiritual or temporal. When in the course of the late eleventh century the cardinals displaced the older Roman officials in ecclesiastical administration, for example in the chancery and the apostolic *camera,* the curial cardinals gradually became the supreme organ of papal government. In the twelfth century the Roman synods ceased to function. And, later, Innocent III "at last provided a basis in legal theory for what had long been a matter of constitutional fact—namely, that the proper business of the cardinals was to assist in governing the affairs of the Universal Church."[46] But the consistory remained consultative in function, since by law it was not a legislative body. Still, its counsels carried weight in view of the moral prestige of its members; and their unanimous opinion invariably prevailed. On the whole, the consistory rendered invaluable service as an advisory tribunal, but only so long as its members were devoted to the interests of the whole Church; when, as often happened in the late Middle Ages, the cardinals were motivated by self-centered interest, the consistory became a scandal.

The heart of papal administration was the chancery, the center in which all legal documents[47] touching on the interests of the Holy See at home and abroad were prepared, and from which they were dispatched throughout the world. Normally it was headed by a cardinal as chancellor or vice-chancellor who was virtually a secretary of state. Here the growing influence of the cardinals can be measured. In the eleventh century the signatures of curial cardinals are first found on the papal bulls (*privilegia maiora*). In the pontificates of Victor II (1055–57), Nicholas II (1058–61) and Alexander II (1061–73), they signed only occasionally; rarely did they sign under Gregory VII.

With the anti-pope Clement III (1080–1100) and Pope Urban II (1088–99) their signatures appear frequently and soon it became normal chancery procedure for the papal bulls to be signed both by the pope and by the cardinals according to a very precise pattern arranged in the pontificate of Innocent II (1130–43). This diplomatic development shows the growing importance of the curial cardinals in papal administration. These cardinals—some of them simple priests or in lesser orders, some mere clerics—were becoming virtually co-administrators with the pope of the universal Church *in urbe et orbe*. As they increased in prestige, the influence of the bishops decreased.

Until the end of the thirteenth century the number of cardinals was rarely more than fifteen, at times less. Because they were the papal electors, the backbone therefore of the continuity of the papacy, they were men of considerable influence in Christendom. Because they were so few in number, and because from their number the pope was elected, their *collegium* was a veritable élite of power and esteem. They were frequently used by the pope as his special ambassadors, *legati a latere,* to dispatch business in the most remote parts of Christendom; and, as legates, they were shielded and protected by the honor and dignity of the apostolic see itself.[48] The different opinions current in the canonical writing of the twelfth and thirteenth centuries strikingly represent their ascendancy in the Church.[49] Thus, for example, Petrus de Vinea, the chancellor of Frederick II held "the principle that the cardinals shared in the authority of the Apostolic See and that, accordingly, they should be admitted to *equa participatio* in the transaction of

Church business."[50] Taken not individually but collectively, the cardinals were considered to be equal, even superior in power to the pope. Therefore, he was bound to consult them before acting. With him they formed a corporation, a body of which he was the head, they the members. His power they shared, but his did not exceed theirs. The cardinals were believed by some to have the right to call a general council to depose the pope if there should be need, while the pope could not depose them apart from a council. Because they were the electoral body of the papacy, they possessed *sede vacante* the supreme power which they conferred. When the pope died, the Church was headed by the *collegium cardinalium*.[51]

Considerations such as these, while not representing the canon law itself, show that the *Curia Romana* had become a power block in the Church with which Christendom had to reckon. By the middle of the twelfth century the cardinals had assumed heraldistic arms and their own standards. By the middle of the next century Innocent IV (1243-54) had granted them the use of 'the red hat' in imitation of the imperial German *Fürsten*. Parallel to the accumulation of external honors and dignities runs their increase in wealth and power. And by virtue of the persuasive pressure which they could bring to bear on the pope they were able to control the quantity and quality of the membership of the college so as to preserve it small in number and selective in character.[52]

The disputed election of 1159, terminating in the schism of the anti-pope Victor IV (1159-64) and his successors against Alexander III (1159-81), was rooted in a political division within the college itself. The crisis led Emperor Frederick I to assume the office of supreme arbitrator between the two papal claimants. At a synod in Pavia in 1160 he judicated the difficult matter in favor of Victor IV whom he personally favored; but in Pope Alexander, the astute canonist Rolando Bandinelli, he was confronted by an opponent far too shrewd and knowledgeable not to see here the imminent danger of the papacy's lapsing back into the jungle of imperial patronage. The fierce contest between pope and emperor which lasted almost twenty years was peacefully concluded at Venice in 1177. The victory was Alexander's. At the Third Lateran Council the pope issued a decree, *Licet de vitanda* (1179), which definitively regulated the canonical procedure to be followed in papal elections. All the cardinals of all orders were legally constituted the papal electors and a two-thirds majority of their votes was specified as necessary for valid election. All others—people, clergy and emperor—were excluded from the election simply, clearly and absolutely.

When Clement IV died in 1268, the sixteen cardinals who assembled to elect his successor vividly demonstrated the frightening extent to which the Church and her well-being depended on them. For three years they failed to produce the votes required for a valid election. They failed because their personal interests were divided along divergent lines and because their historical vision was dim. Certainly they do not seem to have sensed the analogy between the disasters which were befalling the empire during the *Interregnum* (1256–73) and damages which the Church was suffering from this prolonged state of *sede vacante* maintained by their stubbornness. Only after the people of Viterbo had pulled down the roof of the palace in which these self-willed cardinals were gathered, after they were reduced almost to starvation, did they appoint a committee of six to act in the name of all. Their choice fell on the saintly Tedaldo Visconti, archdeacon of Liège, who was neither priest nor cardinal. At the moment (Sept. 1, 1271) he was in the Holy Land. The Church, therefore, remained without a pope for seven more months, until he had returned to Rome, was ordained, consecrated and finally crowned on March 27, 1272. He took the name Gregory X.

To prevent a recurrence of the scandal caused by this three-year vacancy in the Holy See, Pope Gregory approved the decree, *Ubi periculum* (1274), of the Second Council of Lyons, which set up a rigid conclave order aimed at forcing an early election. For it was becoming increasingly clear that the cardinals as papal electors could be a real threat to the welfare of the Church. In the conclaves of the late Middle Ages it became more and more common for the cardinals to augment their power by demanding that the *papabilis* swear to observe a 'capitulation' in return for his election. This sordid legal instrument was aimed at forcing the candidate into granting certain personal privileges to his electors in gratitude for their votes. Most concretely it represents the attempt of the college of cardinals as an oligarchy to restrict the latitude of papal power, to bend it in their favor as an élite. After the conclave of 1352 which elected Innocent VI it was repeated frequently, for example in the conclaves of 1394, 1404, 1406, and so on down into the sixteenth century. This was an abuse, recognized as such, but incorrigible because there was no (still is no) machinery for efficiently handling problems of this kind.

The departure of the popes to Avignon is rooted in causes too complicated to be discussed here. Far from Rome, for almost seventy years, from 1309 to 1377, the papacy remained in this unfortunate exile—the so-called Babylonian Captivity—in circumstances which were far from becoming to its universal office. The scars accumulated in those days still remain. Of the seven popes who occupied the Chair of St. Peter during this period, five were lawyers.[53] It is not surprising, therefore, that legalism characterizes this epoch of papal history. For at this time the centralization which developed under Gregory VII was methodically reduced to a vast bureaucracy reaching out to all parts of the Church. The *Corpus Iuris Canonici* now came into its own in a most special way. It became "not merely an instrument which men use, but . . . a law which they all serve." In the person of John XXII (1316–1334), one of the most astute organizers and financial wizards ever to occupy the papal throne, the whole Church was realigned as a comprehensive, financial and legal system in which every last holder of an ecclesiastical benefice was responsible directly to the Holy See. Courts, lawyers, judges, bureaus, legalities and every manner of legal appurtenance multiplied. Tax money from all parts of the world flowed into Avignon where much of it found its way into the coffers of the curial cardinals whose personal wealth became fabulous.[54] In the midst of the intricate legal web which John XXII had spun sat the *Curia* as the core of the executive, legislative and judicial departments of the Holy See.

The scandal which this handful of French cardinals created at Avignon escaped no one. Not only was their personal and public life with the glittering display of position and wealth a cause of grave concern, but even more than that was the realization that their accumulated power and influence—their independence face to face with the Church—could be neither checked nor reformed by anyone. The signs of the future were ominous to those whose eyes were open; the expectations of even the most cynical would not be disappointed.

On January 17, 1377 Gregory XI returned to Rome where he re-established the papacy in its rightful home after its long exile in Avignon. Somewhat more than a year later, on March 27, 1378, he was dead; and within a matter of days, on April 7th, sixteen cardinals—eleven French, four Italians and one Spaniard—entered what was to prove one of the most stormy, hysterical conclaves in the history of the Church. All through the night of April 7/8 violent mobs of wild Romans, excited by wine and delirious with enthusiasm, stormed about the palace in which the election was taking place. Under threat of reprisal they demanded that a Roman, at least an Italian, be elected; and on more than one occasion during the long vigil they burst into the conclave and menaced the frightened cardinals. The story is well-known and needs no detailed repetition.[55]

Early in the morning of April 8th Bartolomeo Prignani, the archbishop of Bari, was elected *in absentia*. Notified, he accepted, was acknowledged by the cardinals, and acclaimed by the people on April 9th. On Easter Sunday, April 18th, he was crowned as Urban VI in St. Peter's in the presence of the sacred college. No member of it, with the one exception of Cardinal Orsini, suggested that the election had been invalidated by the excessive fear which the mobs had generated in the conclave. Even weeks after the events of these tempestuous days the election of Urban VI remained undisputed.

But the point of interest here is this. By their later repudiation of this pope the cardinals—twenty-three in number—were able to throw Christendom into a state of confusion such as it had never before experienced. Before the mischief of the cardinals of 1378 had run its full course, the Church would be almost brought to the ground. Soon it became evident to the cardinals that in electing Prignani they had been seriously deceived; he was no friend of the *Curia,* he was harsh, irascible, probably unbalanced mentally, bent on reforming the college with a rod of iron, and out of sympathy with the traditions of Avignon. Thereupon, the cardinals left him isolated and cut off. Alleging fear as the invalidating cause of the election of Urban, they deserted him 'as no pope.' But the words which Cardinal Robert of Geneva addressed to Urban VI are most revealing: "Unlike your predecessors, Holy Father, you do not treat the cardinals with that honor which you owe them. You are diminishing our authority, but verily I tell you that we will do our best to diminish yours."[56] It was clear that curial power, if thwarted in its purpose, would clash with papal authority; but it was not yet clear how devastating the clash would be.

On September 20th the cardinals, now assembled in cold resentment at Fondi, entered the conclave and elected their thirty-six year old colleague and leader, Robert of Geneva, who took the name Clement VII. On June 20, 1379 he sailed for France, for distant Avignon, where, surrounded by the recalcitrant cardinals, he set up his papal court. Urban's answer to these schismatic maneuvers was the creation of new cardinals. and the proud and steadfast maintenance of his court at Rome. Thus a double papal obedience, Avignon and Rome, was created as the result of the resentment of a powerful, stubborn minority of churchmen whose personal feelings were made to transcend the common good of Christendom. The scandal was enormous, seeing that it was the work of those men who were commonly believed to be the hinges (*cardines*) on which the whole world turned. But it was the inevitable result of a constitutional deficiency which placed vast power in the hands of a small minority responsible to God alone.[57] Its abuse would depend on the personal quality of its holders.

The scandal of the year 1378/79 grew into the Great Western Schism in which two (later three) popes with their own curial cardinals presided over segments of a divided Christendom. With the election (Nov. 30, 1406) of Angelo Corrario as Gregory XII the first signs of healing the schism appeared. For this new pope of the Roman obedience had twice sworn that he would abdicate on the condition that his rival at Avignon, the eccentric Pedro de Luna, Benedict XIII, do the same. Then the cardinals of both obediences could proceed unimpeded to the election of a new pope whom Christendom would accept unanimously. When the plan failed—as every plan since 1378 had failed—both popes were deserted by almost all their dissatisfied cardinals. By June 29, 1408, fourteen of them—six of Benedict XIII's obedience and eight of Gregory XII's—appealed to a general council to put the disrupted Church in order. This was to be *the* hour of the college of cardinals, when it truly would preside over the destinies of

Christendom. The Council had been called without the popes, might even act against them, but would be under the control of and in consort with the cardinals. On March 25, 1409 the Council opened at Pisa.[58] On June 5th both Gregory XII and Benedict XIII were denounced and deposed as "schismatics, the approvers and makers of schism, notorious heretics, guilty of perjury and violation of solemn promises and openly scandalizing the Church." Their deposition was greeted with a solemn *Te Deum*. After an eleven-day conclave, on June 26th, Peter Philarghi, the archbishop of Milan, was elected Alexander V. But the two deposed popes gave no recognition to the competency of either this council or conclave, while Alexander V obviously refused to recognize the validity of his rivals. The result, therefore, was a triple obedience to which the Church was submitted.

The Council of Constance (1414–18) was convoked to reestablish unity in the Church by electing one supreme pontiff who would replace the multiplicity of claimants. In his hands would be placed the obedience of all Christendom. The conciliar proceedings at Constance show a marked decline in the college of cardinals. Despite its powerful position in the Church its prestige had sunk low. In the eyes of the majority of the bishops and the other ecclesiastics who attended the council, the cardinals were the culprits who had initially brought schismatic misery on the Church, augmented it at their Pisan council, and maintained it out of considerations of self-interest. When, after the elimination of Benedict XIII, Gregory XII and John XXIII, the council finally proceeded to the election of the pope of unity, it resolved in a spirit of resentment that the cardinals should not enjoy the exclusive right of electors. In the conclave, therefore, in which Martin V (1417–31) was elected on November 11, 1417, representatives of the Nations also cast votes. Their presence was deliberately designed to outweigh the influence of the Italian cardinals, who predominated in the conclave.[59] The reform mandates which the different Nations presented to the newly elected pope contained petitions on the renewal of the college, especially on the internationalizing of its membership, on the quality and quantity of its members, and on their style of life.[60] Practically everyone at Constance knew what a dilemma this handful of men presented to the Church.

But like most of the reform measures of the fifteenth century the program of Constance was ineffectual. The issues were too profound to be resolved even by an ecumenical council. It would not be accurate to say that after Constance the *Curia* remained in *status quo;* rather its decline changed in both direction and intensity. For in the latter half of the fifteenth century an uncontrolled nepotism, so much a part of the Renaissance papacy, entered deeply into the life of the *Curia* where in the already existing centralization and bureaucracy it found a fertile field for growth and expansion. Central now was not personal, but familial abuse. For in the age of the great papal families, the Borgias, the Medicis and the della Roveres, ecclesiastical and familial interests were interlaced as a policy. Within the conclaves of this epoch the 'capitulations' as signed and sealed pacts point invariably towards the interests of the curial family. The history of the unfortunate Sixtus IV (1471–84) and his eleven nephews and two nieces is too well-known to require repetition here.[61] Ever tighter and closer the circle of cardinals grew; ever stronger and more inveterate its hold over the Holy See. That Leo X (1513–21) was forced to break the power of the college by the creation (July 1, 1517) of thirty-one new cardinals is significant.[62]

One need not wonder that the saintly, learned, reforming pope Adrian VI (1522–23), in a moment of grave crisis, wrote these words in his *Instructio* for the legate Chieregati at the Diet of Nürnberg:[63]

We all, prelates and clergy, have gone astray from the right way, and for long there is none that has done good; no, not one. To God, therefore, we must give all the glory and humble ourselves before Him; each one of us must consider how he has fallen and be more ready to be judged by God in the day of His wrath. Therefore, in our name, give promises that we shall use all diligence to reform before all things the Roman *Curia,* whence, perhaps, all these evils have had their origin. Thus healing will begin at the source of the sickness.

The *Consilium de emendanda Ecclesia* from the pontificate of Paul III (1534–49) shows that even almost fifteen years after the *Instructio* and twenty years after the publication of Luther's theses, the *Curia* had not been reformed.[64] It remained one of the most sensitive areas of ecclesiastical life.

The Council of Trent in many important respects purified the Church. By eliminating outstanding abuses that had accumulated over the centuries it strengthened and prepared her to face the hard centuries ahead. But it by-passed the problem of the inner renewal of her administrative structure, of the external framework in which she accomplishes her mission in this world. It accomplished no ecclesial renovation. The old forms, cleansed and envigorated, perdured. Despite the Reformation, the Counter-Reformation, the French Revolution and the *Risorgimento,* the *Curia* survived. Neither its power, dignity nor style and practice were very much changed by the circumstances of the world changing about it. It was still 'the senate of the Roman Pontiff' and, therefore, of the universal Church. It is today as much a part of Catholic life as it was two centuries before the discovery of America.

Between the closing of the Council of Trent in 1563 and the opening of the Second Vatican Council in 1962, through the past four hundred years, the constitutional structure of the Church has remained substantially unchanged. It is partly evangelical, partly medieval: monarchical (papacy) by the will of Christ, collegial (cardinalate) by the disposition of history. The revision of this imposing structure is the delicate constitutional problem about which the Second Vatican Council has been so deeply concerned. And here we see that the central issue is not simply the creation of the collegial factor in the Church, as if it had never existed there before, but rather the contest of an already firmly entrenched college (the cardinals) against the pretensions of a new college (the bishops). Will the episcopal order, rooted in the Gospel and holy orders, truly prevail over the cardinalate, rooted in law and history? And if it should, will history be so cruel as to repeat itself in that this new episcopal college in the course of time will develop into an aristocracy, an oligarchy, an exclusive group of ecclesiastical administrators? Will the bishops one day despite their obligation to collegiality surrender their universal vocation in favor of particularism and personalism?

NOTES

[1] The charges against the Christians were manifold: e.g., atheism, Oedipean orgies involving incest, indecency and immorality, Thyestian banquets or cannibalistic infanticide, *lèse majesté,* superstition, magic, sun-worship, onolatry, hatred of the human race. *The True Discourse (ca.* 178) of the pagan Celsus is an epitome of the position against the Church. Cf. H. Chadwick, *Origen: Contra Celsum* (Cambridge 1953).

[2] The expression is Tertullian's, *De anima* 43.

[3] Cf. *Laus Maximi et Quales ducendae sint uxores* 3. The translation is by W. J. Burghardt, S.J., "The Body of Christ: Patristic Insights," in Robert S. Pelton, ed., *The Church as the Body of Christ* (Notre Dame 1963), pp. 75–76.

[4] Cf. the *Passio Santorum Scillitanorum,* July 17, 180, in Africa. The Christian Speratus addressed the proconsul: "If you will give me a quiet hearing, I will tell you the mystery of simplicity." Cf. J. Stevenson, *A New Eusebius* (London 1957), p. 42.

[5] Cf. the *Epistle to Diognetus,* in C. J. Barry, ed., *Readings in Church History,* Vol. 1 (Westminster 1960), p. 40.

[6] *Ibid.,* p. 38. At a very early date the Church separated herself from the Montanistic spirit of 'flight from the world.'

[7] *Ibid.,* p. 22.

[8] In his work *On the Unity of the Church* (251) St. Cyprian puts it this way: "You cannot have God for your Father, if you have not the Church for your mother." *Ibid.,* p. 64.

[9] *Ibid.,* p. 22.

[10] Significantly, in the rite of episcopal consecration the first question asked of the candidate is: "Are you willing by word and example to teach the people, for whom you are ordained, those things which you have learned from the Holy Scripture?" And later in the rite he is bidden, "Receive the Gospel, and go and preach it to the people who have been entrusted to you."

[11] Cf. F. Lot, *La fin du monde antique et le début du moyen âge* (Paris 1951), pp. 444 ff.

[12] Cf. J. Stevenson, *op. cit.,* p. 230.

[13] There is no need to exaggerate here. With few exceptions (e.g., Decius and Diocletian) the persecutions were sporadic, local and disorganized.

[14] Tertullian in his *Apologeticus* 32 wrote with possible reference to 2 Thess. 2:7: "There is another and a greater necessity for our offering prayer for the Emperors, in fact for the complete stability of the Empire . . . For we know that a mighty shock impending over the whole earth, in fact the very end of all things threatening dreadful woes, is retarded only by the continued existence of the Roman Empire."

[15] For Constantine the Church, set deep in his structure of the Empire, was to be a fundamental principle of that world-unity over which he hoped to preside. "He certainly felt himself to be the bishop of all mankind, a God-appointed Pope, and Eusebius when he once gave him that name, was hitting the right nail on the head." A. Alföldi, *The Conversion of Constantine and Pagan Rome* (Oxford 1948), p. 35.

[16] His dictatorial mentality comes to the fore in these words directed to the Catholic bishops who would not hold communion with the heretics because this would be against the canons: "Whatever I will, be that esteemed a canon. The bishops of Syria let me thus speak. Either then obey or go into banishment." Cf. B. J. Kidd, ed., *Documents Illustrative of the History of the Church,* Vol. 2 (New York 1923), p. 74.

[17] *Cunctos populos* (Feb. 27, 380). Cf. *ibid.,* p. 97. This decree, if not actually, at least virtually constituted the Catholic Church the imperial church.

[18] Significantly, the medieval historian Otto of Freising (d. 1158), in his *Chronicle of the Two Cities* 5, Prologue, remarked: "But from the time of Theodosius on, because not only the people but the princes, with few exceptions, were Catholic, it seems to me that history turns not on two cities but on one only, which I call the Church."

[19] Note, for example, his dictum in *Contra Auxentium* 36: "The emperor is *within* the Church, not *above* the Church"; and in his *Epistle* 20: "Divine things are not subject to the imperial power . . . The palaces concern the emperor, the churches concern the bishop."

[20] Cf. C. J. Barry, *op. cit.,* pp. 147–48.

[21] Cf. *Annales Regni Francorum,* a. 749. Pepin's question, "Is it good or not good that the kings in France do not have royal power?" implied more than it expressed. Zachary took the initiative.

[22] C. Dawson, *The Making of Europe* (New York 1952), p. 210, sums up

Boniface's apostolate in these striking words: He was "a man who had a deeper influence on the history of Europe than any Englishman who has ever lived."

[23] This is the first recorded instance of the sacral anointing of a Frankish king. The rite as such did not at the time exist in the traditional liturgy of the Church.

[24] On August 6, 1806 Emperor Francis II (since 1804 Emperor Francis I of Austria) resigned the imperial, Germanic-Roman, dignity. Thus the Holy Roman Empire of the German Nation came to an end.

[25] Cf. S. Ehler and J. B. Morrall, *Church and State through the Centuries* (London 1954), p. 12.

[26] Otto III (983–1002), the father of *Renovatio imperii Romanorum,* endowed bishops with whole counties. Investiture in its formal sense commenced with Henry III (1039–56).

[27] John XII, Octavian, the son of Alberic II, was elected in his eighteenth year. He was a typical licentious, undisciplined young Roman nobleman.

[28] For example, of the twenty-five popes between 955 and 1057 five were deposed by the German emperor and twelve either installed or elected under his influence.

[29] Cf. S. Ehler and J. B. Morrall, *op. cit.,* pp. 25–28.

[30] This was done at the suggestion of Hildebrand. Cf. A. Mirgeler, *Mutations of Western Christianity* (New York 1964), p. 157. Significantly the word *tiara* designating the papal crown is first verifiable in connection with Gregory's close successor Paschal II (1099–1118).

[31] Cf. G. Tellenbach, *Church, State and Christian Society* (Oxford 1940), p. 184.

[32] Note, for example, the letter (Sept. 1075) of Gregory to Henry IV: "But because we do desire to enjoy that peace which is to be had in Christ, not only with you whom God has set at the height of human affairs, but with all men, and to respect the rights of each individual, we greatly desire to stand with you in heart and mind." Cf. *Registrum* 3, 7.

[33] Cf. for example his rebuke to Archbishop Liemar of Bremen (*Reg.* 2, 28) and his citation of Bishop Otto of Constance to Rome (*Reg.* 2, 29).

[34] Cf. his letter (*Reg.* 2, 49) to Hugo of Cluny.

[35] Cf. S. Ehler and J. B. Morrall, *op. cit.,* pp. 43–44. Note by way of contrast how Pope Gregory I (d. 604) refused the title *papa universalis* in favor of 'servant of the servants of God' and benignly tolerated a diversity of rites, while Gregory VII claimed to be 'universal bishop' and worked for liturgical uniformity in the Church.

[36] Translated by E. Emerton, *The Correspondence of Pope Gregory VII* (New York 1932).

[37] Cf. *ibid.,* pp. 64–65. Gregory wrote to his friend Hugo of Cluny, asking sympathy for the burdens of his office: "A vast and universal grief and sadness walls me about . . . I am crushed by a thousand woes, and suffer a living death. . . ."

[38] Cf. *Reg.* 2, 63, where he wrote to Duke Geisa of Hungary: "We are sure that you know that the kingdom of Hungary, as all other kingdoms, must be free and subject to the king of no other kingdom save the holy and universal mother, the Church of Rome, which does not regard its subjects as servants but receives all of them as sons." Cf. J. P. Whitney, *Hildebrandine Essays* (Cambridge 1932), pp. 57–58.

[39] Note, for example, Gregory's remark to Hermann of Metz: "Who does not know that kings and princes derive their origin from men ignorant of God who raised themselves above their fellows by pride, plunder, treachery, murder—in short, by every kind of crime—at the instigation of the Devil, the prince of this world . . . ?" Cf. E. Emerton, *op. cit.,* p. 169.

[40] Gregory VII died at Salerno on May 25, 1085. His last words empitomize his life: "I have loved justice and hated iniquity. Therefore, I die in exile."

[41] For example, according to Cardinal Zabarella (d. 1417) the Holy See, which is the Church, is "constituted by the pope and the cardinals who become, metaphorically speaking, members of the pope's body." Cf. W. Ullmann, *The Origins of the Great Schism* (London 1948), p. 203.

[42] Cf. K. Jordan, "Die Entstehung der römischen Kurie," *Savigny-Zeitschrift für Rechtsgeschichte* 59, *Kan. Abt.,* 28 (1939), p. 127.

[43] *Contra philargyriam* 7 (*PL* 145, 540B). Cf. S. Kuttner, "Cardinalis: the History of a Canonical Concept," *Traditio* 3 (1945), pp. 129–214. The present code of canon law, canon 230, preserves the same concept of the cardinalate.

[44] *Contra philargyriam* 7 (*PL* 145, 540B).

[45] Cf. K. Jordan, *op. cit.,* pp. 125 ff.

[46] B. Tierney, *Foundations of the Conciliar Theory* (Cambridge 1955), p. 95.

[47] Cf. R. L. Poole, *The Papal Chancery* (Cambridge 1915).

[48] W. Plöchl, *Geschichte des Kirchenrechts,* Vol. 3 (Vienna 1961), pp. 110–111.

[49] Cf. B. Tierney, *op. cit.,* "Pope and Cardinals," Chap. 3, pp. 68–84.

[50] *Ibid.,* p. 78.

[51] *Ibid.,* pp. 73 ff.

[52] Note the stipulations made at a later date in the conclave that elected

Innocent VI (d. 1362) at Avignon. Cf. G. Mollat, *The Popes at Avignon* (New York 1963), pp. 44–45.

[53] Clement V, Clement VI, John XXII, Innocent VI and Gregory XI.

[54] "So John XXII, in 1316, and Benedict XII, in 1334, divided up 100,000 florins between the cardinals. Clement VI, in 1342, gave them 108,000; Innocent VI, 75,000 in 1352; Urban V, ten years later, only 40,000." Cf. P. Hughes, *A History of the Church,* Vol. 3 (New York 1947), p. 158.

[55] It is best told by W. Ullmann in his work cited in n. 41 *supra.*

[56] *Ibid.,* p. 186.

[57] In this period the constitutional point of view of the cardinals is pronouncedly oligarchic. Cf. *ibid.,* pp. 186 ff.

[58] In answer to the convocation of the ecumenical council by the cardinals, Gregory XII and Benedict XIII summoned their own councils, the one at Cividale, the other at Perpignan, which, though failures, helped to sustain the universal confusion.

[59] Under the auspices of the council, the composition of the conclave consisted of the twenty-three cardinals of the three obediences plus thirty delegates, six from each of the five Nations. The election was to depend on two-thirds of the votes of each group.

[60] The concordats of the Germans, the French and the English explicitly recommended such a renewal to the newly elected pope.

[61] "Of his eleven nephews six were clerics—it was a simple matter to make five of them cardinals, while the sixth became Bishop of Ferrara and Patriarch of Antioch . . . A sixth red hat went to one of his niece's sons." Cf. P. Hughes, *op. cit.,* Vol. 3, pp. 389–90.

[62] Leo was prompted to this drastic reform by the sad state of the secularization of the college initiated by Sixtus IV. Unfortunately his choices for the cardinalate were also prompted by financial considerations. Cf. L. Pastor, *The History of the Popes,* Vol. 7 (St. Louis 1908), pp. 196 ff.

[63] Cf. C. Mirbt, *Quellen zur Geschichte des Papsttums und des Römischen Katholizismus* (Tübingen 1914), p. 261; and R. E. McNally, S.J., *The Reform of the Church* (New York 1963), pp. 115–116.

[64] Cf. R. E. McNally, S.J., *ibid.,* pp. 120–21.

3 * Bible

HOLY SCRIPTURE, GOD'S WORD, IS fundamental to Christianity. For the life of the Church as a worshipping and believing community is sustained both by "grace and truth." Her life, therefore, centers about Worship, which sanctifies, and Word, which enlightens. The sacred books, her books *par excellence,* contain the saving *evangelium,* "the good news of salvation," in which all men are invited to share. This is the true vocation of the Church—to disseminate the Gospel to all the nations of the earth and in this world-wide apostolate to serve as Christ's special pedagogue. At each moment of her history she must be ready and able to impart the salutary lessons which she has learned from her Lord. She must, therefore, understand the truths which she is to teach, know how to communicate them, and reflect them in the historical greatness of her own life.

To teach the Word of God universally is the Church's chal-

lenge. It is not however overwhelming, since the Church does
not work alone. In the exercise of her *magisterium* she enjoys
the assistance of the Spirit as well as the support of the faithful. As teacher, she is especially assisted by biblical exegesis
whose function is to open up the meaning of the sacred text.
For the light which this science throws on the Christian mystery and its inner relation to Christian life illuminates the
Church and her faithful. The liturgy also serves the *magisterium*. It proclaims the Word of God in a sacral atmosphere,
and thus introduces Holy Scripture in an intimate way into
the prayer life of the Church. God's Word is a special food
which religiously nourishes the heart and mind of those who
believe it. Because it is the foundation of theology and worship
without which Christians cannot live, its centrality in the
religious life of the faithful can never be a matter of indif-
ference. In this world the Church is the dispenser of that
"grace and truth" which "came through Jesus Christ."[1]

Bible science is subject to the flow of culture. Under the
pressure of history, it is distinctly marked by the *Zeitgeist*. Thus
every cultural epoch in Church History has produced an understanding of Holy Scripture which in some way is characteristic
of that era. In fact, in her biblical literature the rising and
falling fortunes of the Church over the centuries can be traced
with clarity. For in a sense exegesis is a mirror reflecting
Christian life and piety at different historical moments; it is
also a precious source book of valuable insights into the theological development of the Church.[2] A survey of ecclesiastical
history conveys the distinct impression that whenever the level
of biblical exegesis falls low, whenever the reading of Holy

Scripture is neglected, the Church suffers in all vital areas—spiritual, liturgical, ecclesial and theological. When the Bible becomes an esoteric book closed to the faithful, or a book whose essential message is misread, a religious crisis is prepared. By the end of the Middle Ages precisely such a crisis—a biblical crisis—had been reached. The history of the Reformation shows that the ultimate resolution of this critical problem almost brought the whole Christian Church to ruin.

The Christians of the early Church were Bible-minded. The Church of the Martyrs found a special consolation in the Book of Psalms which she incorporated into divine worship. In the center of this book she discovered Christ, His Church and His People.[3] The early catechumenate was based on a *catechesis* which largely consisted in Bible-study; and the faithful who assembled on the Lord's Day were invariably instructed by their bishop in Holy Scripture whose central lesson was love of God and man.[4] In fact, a considerable portion of divine service in the early Church was devoted to Bible-reading. And in this ancient period the Christian community was privileged to hear the Word of God in its mother tongue rather than in an archaic language. The existence of Greek, and, later, Latin translations of Scripture indicates the concern of the Church from the apostolic age onward that God's Word be transmitted in a living language.[5] For in her pedagogy the people were educated in close, direct acquaintance with the sacred text itself. The sources of the history of the ancient Church show how pronouncedly biblical was her profession of Christ.

Thus Origen (d. 253) exhorts his hearers to a knowledge of

Scripture in a passage which in many respects is an epitome of the mind of the primitive Church on the Bible:[6]

Let us keep the Scriptures in mind and mediate upon them day and night, persevering in prayer, always on watch. Let us beg the Lord to give us real knowledge of what we read and to show us not only how to understand it, but how to put it into practice, so that we may deserve to obtain spiritual grace, enlightened by the law of the Holy Spirit, through Jesus Christ Our Lord, whose power and glory will endure throughout the ages. Amen.

And somewhat later we find the same spirit in a letter of St. Gregory the Great (d. 604) in which he sternly rebukes the imperial physician Theodorus for neglecting "to read daily the words of his Redeemer."[7]

For what is Scripture, save a missive of Almighty God to His creatures? . . . The emperor of heaven, the Lord of men and angels, has transmitted to you for your life His letters, and despite that, honorable son, you neglect to read them with eagerness. Study, I beseech you, and every day read meditatively the words of your Creator.

Throughout patristic literature the Bible dominates not as a learned book, not as a source book for the spiritual life, but as a deposit of interior knowledge of Christ "whose unique character illumines the entire breadth of human life and 'the almighty God' who has created all and who 'calls mankind to the joy of eternal life.' "[8]

The earliest writings of both the Greek and Latin Fathers

of the Church with their copious citations from Scripture presuppose an audience familiar with the sacred text; and their sermons, generally delivered to the people in a liturgical setting, are distinctly biblical in quality. The renowned preachers of the ancient Church were often distinguished bishops such as St. Ambrose (d. 397) and St. Augustine (d. 430); and, in many instances, their sermons form a continuous commentary on the text of Holy Scripture.[9] Patristic theology is distinctly biblical in spirit. For the theologian was an exegete, and exegesis was theology.[10] The bishops, therefore, as theologians, were fundamentally preoccupied with the Bible; as pastors, their concern was with preaching the Word of God. Their sermons on the great themes of salvation history were meaningful to their hearers. For these chief pastors were both well acquainted with the needs of the people entrusted to their pastoral care and deeply instructed in the Bible as the Church's own book. While the office of preaching belonged to the bishop as a man of piety, knowledge and authority, the reading of Scripture in the assembly was reserved to the deacon and the lector to insure its reverent, competent transmission. Thus the people were fed at the Lord's table with the bread of life—His Word and Sacrament.

The art of the early Church drew its inspiration from the Bible. Here, for example, in the frescoes of the catacombs and in the plastic representations on the sarcophaguses the inner mind of the Christian can be clearly read. Baptism is a washing. The Church is a mother. The Eucharist is a food. Life is a pilgrimage. Death is a sleep. Heaven is a banquet. Old and New Testament personages such as Adam and Eve, Cain and Abel,

Abraham and Isaac, Daniel, Mary the Mother of Jesus, Peter and Paul, Lazarus, the four evangelists, and others, are so represented that the parallel significance of the two Testaments in the totality of salvation history is unmistakable. The lesson is constant. The Old Testament receives its prophetic fulfillment in the New Testament.[11] In this ancient art Christ is portrayed as Lord and Redeemer of men, the King of Glory, the celestial Mediator. Above all He is the Good Shepherd, who calls His own sheep by name, protects them from the hireling and leaves the ninety-nine to find the one.[12] All—the law and the prophets—is made to converge in the *Christos* represented with radiant majesty and biblical serenity as He presides over the destiny of mankind.

Both the public and private prayers of the early Christians were biblical in language and content. For example, the prayer which St. Irenaeus of Lyons (d. *ca.* 202) offered before his martyrdom, "is made to the Father, who was revealed in the old law as well as in the new. The idea of continuity in God's scheme of salvation, as it unfolds in the course of history," was favored by him:[13]

I appeal to you, Lord, God of Abraham, God of Isaac, God of Jacob and Israel, you the Father of our Lord Jesus Christ. Infinitely merciful as you are, it is your will that we should learn to know you. You made heaven and earth. You rule supreme over all that is. You are the true, only God. There is no other god above you. Through our Lord Jesus Christ. . . .

The prayers which have come down to us from the ancient Church are objectively formulated. A certain real strength and dignity come from the theological and biblical foundation on which they rest. Here the sentimental, the romantic and the imaginative, which become prominent at a later stage in the development of prayer-forms, do not intrude.

In the eyes of the Roman Empire the Bible was an essential element of the Christian community. It paralleled even the hierarchic structure of the Church in importance. And both were the object of emperor Diocletian's (284–305) furious persecution which broke out in the early Spring of 303. Eusebius[14] reports that "imperial edicts were published everywhere, commanding that the churches be levelled to the ground and the Scriptures be destroyed by fire, and ordering that those who held places of honor be degraded." And Lactantius[15] assures us that "the books of the Holy Scriptures were found, and they were committed to the flames." The sinister demand which the Roman magistrate made of the Christians of Cirta on May 19, 303, was typical:[16] "Bring out the Scriptures that you have so that we can obey the orders and command of the emperors."

As heir to the Christian revelation of Jerusalem, the Greek wisdom of Athens and the Latin empire of Rome, the medieval world rose from the ashes of Antiquity. This precious heritage developed into the characteristic triad, *Sacerdotium, Imperium* and *Studium,* which in the Middle Ages centered in Italy, Germany and France, and which represented the medieval cultural synthesis.[17] But the Middle Ages only partially entered into the rich patrimony of these three capital cities of religion, philosophy and law. For the transition from the ancient to the medieval was violent, harsh, abrupt in a sense, and filled with calamity. In its genesis many diverse factors crossed and criss-crossed; and many extraneous elements entered the life stream of the old cultures, so that in the course of this transformation much of the ancient treasure was lost, destroyed, discarded or distorted. The medieval world, therefore, while enjoying a certain unbroken continuity with the past, is not simply the mature fruit of the ancient civilizations. Its inner character represents a complexity of cultural facets both old and new.

Under the stress of these different influences the religious mode of early Christianity was sharply displaced in another direction. Holy Scripture, for example, as a direct, vital force in the spiritual life of the faithful gradually fell into deep shadow as new religious forms, less biblical but more popular, arose to take its place. In the course of the Middle Ages the Bible became a book weighed down under the heavy burden of tradition. It was arbitrarily interpreted according to a multiplicity of senses—literal and spiritual—rarely available in the vernacular, and almost never known in the original biblical languages. Within the framework of the liturgy—the Mass, the Sacraments and the Office—the Bible was read in Latin, which normally was not understood either by the clergy or the laity, while in the homilies and sermons which were preached to the faithful it scarcely ever received an interpretation that was solidly built on salvation history and biblical theology. The Bible could not, therefore, have played a direct and immediate role in the formation of Christian piety.[18]

Normally in the Middle Ages the contents of Scripture were communicated to the people by the priests. It was indirect transmission in the ratio of reader and hearer. The reproach here is not so much that the Bible was an unknown book (it never was that) but that its function in the spiritual life of the individual Christian was miscalculated. It was not regarded as the voice of Christ bearing witness before all men of all times to His merciful Father in heaven and to His own redemptive mission on earth. It was not the place, as Erasmus put it, where men looked to find "the quick and living image of His most holy mind, yea, and Christ Himself, healing, dying, rising again." It was, rather, a book filled with examples from the life of the Saviour whose overpowering personality moved men to do good and avoid evil. Holy Scripture, therefore, as a factor in medieval religious life, tended more towards the historical and propositional order than the sacramental and the presential.

Yet the medieval man sincerely loved the Bible, even if he did not grasp it in its totality as the recorded history of salvation. The whole atmosphere of his life was permeated with themes drawn from Holy Scripture. The iconography of the Gothic cathedral was biblical to the core; and the book illuminations which have come down to us from this period are dominated by scriptural subjects. The magnificence of the de luxe Bible manuscripts of the Middle Ages argues to a deep reverence for the Word of God. The liturgical year, which played so large a role in everyday medieval life, was also fundamentally biblical. In fact, the Easter (Paschal) and Christmas (Incarnational) cycles were the twin axes on which the commerce of human life turned. And if as the Middle Ages grew older feasts of the saints tended more and more to intrude on their centrality, these two solemnities of the Lord never ceased to be meaningful. Their themes were incorporated into the mystery plays which were viewed with the deepest interest. The Bible was indeed a book of "wondrous profundity" both for the intellectual and the spiritual life.[19] It was cultivated in all monastic centers of learning and commented on by the university masters. In fact, the biblical commentaries which have survived from the Middle Ages form a massive testimonial to the sincere concern of the medieval scholar for the *sacra pagina*.

But despite the impressive position which the Bible occupied in medieval life, its significance in the spiritual life of the individual was not appreciated. And this is the heart of the matter. The character of the influence which it exercised on religious life was out of proportion to its intrinsic excellence. Rarely, if ever, did the medieval Church solemnly exhort the faithful to read the Scriptures as an integral part of their Catholic life and piety. Nor were adequate vernacular translations prepared and disseminated under official auspices and with official blessing. The observation of St. Thomas More (d. 1535) on the lack of an English translation of the Bible is significant:[20]

And surely how it hath happed, that in all this while God hath either not suffered, or not provided, that any good virtuous man hath had the mind in faithful wise to translate it, and thereupon either the clergy, or at the least wise, some one bishop to approve it: this can I nothing tell.

I am sure, quoth the Messenger, ye doubt not but that I am full and whole of your mind in this matter, that the Bible should be in our English tongue. But yet that the clergy is of the contrary, and would not have it so, that appeareth well, in that they suffer it not to be so.

Overawed by its Latin past, the medieval Church clung tenaciously to the Latin Bible, the *Vulgata latina* of St. Jerome, long after it had ceased to be a living language in the Western world.

Until the invention of the printing press in the middle of the fifteenth century, the manual transcription of a Bible codex was a laborious and expensive task.[21] A manuscript Bible, as a massive production of at least two folio volumes on parchment or vellum, was a book which was necessarily rare and very costly. This relative scarcity of the Bible cannot in justice be imputed to the Church. It was, rather, contingent on the cultural development of the contemporary world. For the common people the Bible was a closed book, and necessarily so, since they were too poor to purchase so extraordinary an item; and had they had the good fortune to possess one, they would have been too illiterate to read it. Nor could the ordinary parish priests read the Latin Vulgate with ease and ready comprehension, since the majority of them were not university educated. Giraldus Cambrensis' (d. 1223) list of the various blunders which parish priests of his day had committed in reading the Latin text of the Scripture shows how compelling was the need of a vernacular translation of the Bible which could be accessible to clergy and laity alike.[22]

A letter of Innocent III (d. 1218) to the Church of Metz is of interest for the important insight which it yields into the official attitude towards Scripture-reading by the laity. It appears from this letter of July 21, 1199 that a rather large group of Bible-reading men and women, "largely motivated by a desire of understanding Scripture," had formed themselves into an esoteric circle to read the Scripture together in French translations which they had made, to preach to one another and to discuss various biblical themes. Contending that "they had better in their own books," they contemptuously rejected "the simplicity of their priests," their sermons and their admonitions. Alerted to this curious situation, Pope Innocent replied by rebuking their exclusive and rebellious spirit. While he praised as a general principle the "desire to understand Scripture and the zeal to preach according to it," he found the situation in Metz exceptional. It showed an independence of ecclesiastical authority that was in all probability inspired by Waldensian principles. The pope's conclusion brings out clearly the character of medieval reverence for the "wondrous profundity" of Scripture:[23]

The hidden mysteries of the faith are not to be indiscriminately opened to all, since they cannot be understood by all indiscriminately, but only by those who can grasp them with a believing mind . . . For the depth of Scripture is so profound that not only the simple and unlettered but also the prudent and learned are not fully capable of explaining its meaning. Wherefore Scripture says: "Many seek and fail in their search." Whence of old it was rightly established in the divine law that, "A beast which had touched the mountain, should be stoned," lest perhaps the simple and the unlearned should presume to attain to the sublimity of Sacred Scripture, or to preach it to others.

In another context the matter is stated this way: Scripture is not for the simple as pearls are not for swine.

In the mentality which underlines this document Holy Scripture is comprehended as an esoteric book. Since not even "the prudent and learned" can grasp its meaning, obviously "the simple and unlettered" should not even try. But, at all events, if uneducated laymen could not understand the Scriptures in a vernacular translation, how were they to understand them in the Latin Vulgate? Or, if the simple laity could not grasp the Scripture, was there any hope that the simple priests could do much better with it?

In another letter of the same date, Innocent III ordered the bishop and chapter of the Church of Metz to inquire into the whole matter for him, to inform him as to "who was the author of this translation, what was his teaching, the faith of those who were using it, the reason for their teaching, whether they venerate the Apostolic See and the Catholic Church. . . ."[24] On December 9th the Cistercian abbots of Citeaux, Morimond and de Crista were appointed by the pope to investigate the case for him. Though he had only censured the use of vernacular versions of the Bible to the extent that such a practice *de facto* was leading to unlicensed preaching and to contempt of the clergy, the abbots saw to it that all the translations of the Bible which they found in this region were summarily burnt. Thus the affairs of Metz (by no means an isolated case) were settled.[25] The biblical circle was broken.

During these centuries no concerted attempt was made by the hierarchy to provide a vernacular version of Scripture which would meet all the tests of orthodoxy. In the course of the Middle Ages various private individuals and groups (for example, the Waldensians and the Lollards) did make translations in whole or in part of the Bible. The Psalms and the Sunday Gospels were also translated into the vernacular by Catholics; and these versions, which were to a certain extent current in orthodox Catholic circles (at least among the better-educated classes), were not forbidden. There is no need here to refute the legend that the Western world had to await the arrival of Martin Luther on the scene to have the privilege of reading the Bible in translation—the evidence is to the contrary.[26] But these medieval versions were never popular in the sense that they were well known by the people. The technical culture of the Middle Ages, as we have remarked above, was not so developed as to permit a wide distribution of books.

The medieval Church did not encourage vernacular versions of its sacred books either biblical or liturgical. Thus, the Synod of Toulouse (1229), acting under the stress of the Albigensian crisis which was then wracking southern France, decreed:[27]

The laity shall not have books of Scripture with the exception of the psalter and the divine office. And they shall not have these books in the vernacular. Moreover, we forbid the laity the permission to have books of the Old or the New Testament, unless for the sake of devotion one should wish to have a psalter or a breviary, or the hours of the Blessed Virgin. But we most strictly prohibit their having these books translated into the vernacular.

Prohibitions of this kind did not prevent translations from being made, at least surreptitiously; but they did help to create the unfortunate image of the Church as an enemy of Holy Scripture, an image whose revision has required centuries of patient instruction and explanation to effect.

The first complete Bible in the English language, the so-called Lollard Bible (1380-84), emerged in the violently anti-papal circle (Nicholas of Hereford and John Purvey) of John Wycliff (d. 1384), 'the morning star of the Reformation.'[28] Its preparation, therefore, was not a project launched under ecclesiastical auspices. Far from that, it was the work of scholars who in their resentment of canon law, hierarchical authority and the Holy See were seeking to lay a new foundation for the Church which they hoped to save. It is bitterly ironic to note that, while the popes (Urban VI and Clement VII) of the Great Western Schism were deeply involved in the defense of their legitimacy, the enemies of the Holy See were producing the first complete English translation of the Word of God as a refutation of the validity of the papacy itself. In view of what has already been said, it is almost unnecessary to point out that this great 'Lollard Bible' was condemned in open, unequivocal terms by ecclesiastical authority.[29]

Medieval exegesis rested on tradition. It was scarcely influenced by biblical history, textual criticisms or ancient philology, for throughout most of the Middle Ages Hebrew and Greek were virtually unknown.[30] Decisive for exegesis was patristic authority, especially that of the great tetrad, Saints Jerome, Ambrose, Augustine and Gregory, who represented *the* voice of Christian tradition. With the passage of time these four Latin Fathers solidified into a corpus of authorities whose prestige was unexcelled. But the patristic theology which the

Middle Ages knew was only grasped incompletely, almost never as a system of thought. For centuries the Greek Fathers had been cut off from the West; and even the Latin Fathers whose works had been transmitted were known only in a fragmentary sort of way. Thus the medieval scholar too often had to rely on *florilegia,* collections of citations (*sententiae*), which had been gathered from patristic works, often without critical reference to their context. Frequently they were transmitted anonymously or even spuriously. But their influence on medieval exegesis was not negligible.[31]

In terms of this prominence of patristic authority, exegesis, especially in the monastic centers where tradition was held in high reverence, tended more and more to become stereotyped, conventional, ordinary and conservative. But in the scholastic circles of learning, particularly after the middle of the twelfth century, dialectic rather than authority became the key for opening up the meaning of the sacred text. This rational approach at first raised a veritable storm in the old monastic schools, because it posed new, modern biblical questions before which traditional exegesis felt inadequate and mute. It was a crisis for the system of biblical exegesis which had been undisputed for more than five hundred years.[32] But at the end of the Middle Ages scholastic exegesis, with very few exceptions (e.g., Nicholas of Lyra), had become progressively less real, more academic and bookish, heavily rational and abstract; imperceptibly it had drifted further and further away from the inspired text whose meaning it was searching. In fact, the theology of the late Middle Ages with its complicated technical structure is scarcely recognizable as a descendant of the earlier patristic theology whose avowed intention was to detect and understand the voice of God speaking in the profundity of His inspired Word.

The most important influence which patristic antiquity exerted on medieval exegesis is to be found in hermeneutics, the norms which govern the interpretation of Holy Scriptures. The medieval exegete accepted the authority of the Fathers[33] and, like them, believed that the text of Sacred Scripture yields a manifold number of senses. For God, as author of Scripture, was believed to have spoken one set of words which simultaneously contained four levels of meaning: the literal (historical) and the spiritual, which in turn is allegorical, tropological and anagogical. This was the tradition of Origen and the Neo-Platonists of Alexandria—intellectual factors of great importance in medieval exegesis.[34] In terms of this ancient tradition it was generally taught that deep beneath the superficial, the apparent, the obvious level of reality, the *historical* for example, was to be found the true reality—the *spiritual*. Just as the macrocosmos was one vast symbol or sacrament both revealing and concealing God, so the *sacra pagina* as a microcosmos involved signs and symbols of higher realities which exegesis was to discover. Beneath 'the letter' was 'the spirit'; and beneath history was allegory, tropology and anagogy, the deepest theological, moral and eschatological sense of the sacred text. To unearth these sacramental treasures of Scripture was the true vocation of the biblical scholar.

This spiritual hermeneutic tended to siphon off and discard the essence of Holy Scripture—the literal sense of God's Word. In the course of the Middle Ages spiritual exegesis became uncontrolled, capricious and imaginative, at times fantastic. It distracted the faithful away from the true significance of the historical aspects of Christianity into a mystical atmosphere of the symbol and the symbolized. The allegorical interpretation of the Bible represents exegesis transcending history and moving on a mystical level exterior to the text itself. If left unchallenged, this theory would have uprooted Christianity from the historical order. For the medieval exegete the deepest and most important sense of the text was the spiritual, which contained the celestial mysteries, the food of the soul. His *point de départ* was indeed the literal and the historical, but his mind ultimately gravitated to the anagogic, the ultimate mystery of the eschatological order.

The following excerpt from the *Summa Gloria* of the obscure Honorius Augustodunensis (*fl. ca.* 1150) is representative both of the method of spiritual exegesis and its application to contemporary problems. Writing at a time when the critical question of the relation of the spiritual to the temporal order was being agitated on all sides, Honorius maintained a decidedly pro-papal position, which, he believed, could be defended from the text of Holy Scripture. This is part of his argument from the opening chapters of Genesis:[35]

. . . Adam begot from his wife two sons, because Christ willed to beget from His spouse, the Church, the clergy and the people. These two sons, Abel and Cain, in their state of life showed forth the two orders, the Priesthood and the Kingship. Abel, the type of the Priesthood: Abel, who was the shepherd of the sheep, typified the Priesthood in which there is pastoral vigilance, inasmuch as it protects the sheep of Christ . . . He was killed by his brother, because Priesthood is overwhelmed frequently by Kingship. Cain, the type of Kingship: Cain, who cultivated the land and built a city over which he ruled, typified the Kingship . . . The Lord, who praises Abel the priest and approves his sacrifice, shows clearly how far the Priesthood excels the Kingship in dignity. He vituperates the king and rejects his gifts. . . .

Thus by the use of allegorical types (stated but not proved) Honorius attempts to demonstrate from Scripture not only that the spiritual authority is superior to the temporal but also that the latter descends from Cain, the father of all homicide in this world. And since the method which Honorius illustrates here was not peculiar to him but common to the greater majority of the biblical exegetes, it is no cause for wonder that the medieval world terminated in a Bible revolution.[36]

The opening years of the sixteenth century teemed with an intellectual ferment which was a curious blend of both the old and the new learning. The *Via antiqua,* the scholastic theology and learning of the Middle Ages, was far from dead. In fact, it was able to produce in the person of Cardinal Cajetan (Thomas de Vio, O.P., d. 1534) a theologian who was one of the most brilliant commentators on the text of St. Thomas. Nor was he the only competent representative of scholastic thought. The theologians of both the Dominican and Franciscan Orders, which at this time enjoyed considerable influence, were to a large extent rooted in this medieval tradition. Their theology in its dialectic subtilty was typical of the late Middle Ages. Formal and essential in approaching the perennial problems, it seemed far removed from the concrete realities of contemporary life. In consequence, the thinkers of the new generation which was growing up felt themselves very much out of harmony with the intellectualism of the old learning; they looked elsewhere, to art, literature, philology and history, for a field of concentration worthy of their talent.

How low theology and theologians had fallen among these new humanists is gathered from the bitter invective which Erasmus heaped upon both in his *Encomium Moriae* (1509):[37]

[The theologians are a] marvellously supercilious and irascible race. For they attack me with six hundred arguments, in squadrons, and drive me to make a recantation; which if I refuse, they will straightway proclaim me an heretic. By this thunderbolt they are wont to terrify any toward whom they are ill disposed. . . . They are happy in their self-love, and as if they already inhabited the third heaven they look down from a height on all other mortal men as on creatures that crawl on the ground, and they come near to pitying them. They are protected by a wall of scholastic definitions, arguments, corollaries, implicit and explicit propositions. . . .

In another place in the same work he describes with sarcastic derision the theological *academica* of his day:[38]

Here [the theologians] rise to the height of theological majesty, sounding in the ears of the audience those august titles of Illustrious Doctor, Subtle Doctor, Supersubtle Doctor, Seraphic Doctor, Holy Doctor, Invincible Doctor. Then they bandy about, before an uneducated crowd, their syllogisms, majors, minors, conclusions, corollaries, conversions, and such bloodless and more than scholastic pedantry . . . They bring in some silly and popular story . . . and interpret it allegorically, tropologically, and anagogically. And in this fashion they complete their chimera. . . .

These words were not written by the Protestant Reformers. On the contrary, they came from the pen of one of the most distinguished humanists of the day, a scholar sought out by both pope and emperor, a savant patronized by the universities, celebrated by Holbein and Dürer, and befriended by the English saints John Fisher and Thomas More (in whose home the *Encomium Moriae,* the source of these citations, was written.)

The early sixteenth century was restless with scholastic theology. In fact, the Aristotelianism which since the thirteenth century had served as her faithful handmaid became the object of most bitter ridicule and scorn. In a series of theses—the so-called *Disputation against Scholastic Theology*—which Martin Luther, while still a Catholic in good standing, prepared for Franz Günther's defense at the University of Wittenberg on September 4, 1517, we read propositions such as these:[39]

It is an error to say that no man can become a theologian without Aristotle. Indeed, no one can become a theologian unless he becomes one without Aristotle.
Briefly, the whole Aristotle is to theology as darkness is to light.

Indeed, when the influential humanist Christopher Scheurl of Nürnberg read these and the other ninety-four theses (couched in a similar vein), he exclaimed that this disputation would "restore the theology of Christ."

Four years later, in an invective against Latomus (Jacobus Masson) of Louvain University, Luther expressed himself more fully and caustically on the subject of scholastic theology:[40]

I think that I have sufficiently shown from their own writings that scholastic theology is nothing else than ignorance of the truth and a stumbling block in comparison with Scripture . . . My advice has been that a young man avoid scholastic philosophy and theology like the very death of his soul . . . How was Christianity taught in the times of the martyrs when this philosophy and theology did not exist? How did Christ himself teach? In all these hundreds of years up to the present, the courses at the universities have not produced out of so many students a single martyr or saint . . . Scholastic philosophy and theology are known from their fruits. I have the strongest doubts as to whether Thomas Aquinas is among the damned or the blessed. . . .

Basic to the anti-scholasticism of Erasmus, Luther and the Christian humanists was their perception that theology in drifting from Scripture and the Fathers (at least, for Erasmus) had become lost in a maze of techniques and technicalities. The new learning stood for a reformation of theology by orientating it around Holy Scripture as its focal point. Thus Luther writes:[41]

Who does not see how the universities read the Bible? Compare what is read and written in the *Sentences* and on philosophy with what they write and teach about the Bible—which ought to flourish and reign as the most important of all—and you will see what place the Word of God has in these seats of higher learning.

Paradoxically, Luther—'the medieval man ushering in the modern age'—was advocating an academic reform which in its insistence on the centrality of the Bible in theology would in a sense carry theological study back to the golden ideal of the early Middle Ages.

Born out of a desire to lead Christian thought in a new direction, the new learning was supported by scholars who had been deeply influenced by the literary and artistic creativity of the Renaissance as a 're-awakening' of Western culture. Many of them were Christian humanists whose interest centered in a revival of theology by awakening it to the best aspects of Hebrew and Greek philology, textual criticism, historical method, ancient Christian literature, history and archeology. In fact, they sponsored a program of return to the sources of Christianity, a program which, if successfully implemented, would have resulted in a reformation of theology, the very heart of the intellectual life of the Church. In a word, these 'philosophers of Christ,' as they called themselves, worked for religious enlightenment or, to use Erasmus' phrase, the *restitutio Christianismi,* by 're-awakening' Catholic theology to the treasures of her ancient past. This meant concretely "an emphasis on the simplicity of truth, the spirituality and inwardness of the religious life, and the imitation of Christ."[42]

The most striking evidence that a new stage in the history of scriptural studies had been reached in the opening years of the sixteenth century is to be found in the renewed interest in the biblical languages, Hebrew and Greek. It is a concrete expression of the formula, 'Back to the sources!' In 1516 Erasmus first published the printed Greek text of the New Testament (or, as he pedantically called it, the *Novum Instrumentum*) with a new Latin translation and a learned commentary on the text. It is prefaced by a gracious dedication to Pope Leo X, "Pontifici modis omnibus Summo," who in his letter of acceptance praised the work as beneficial "to students of sacred theology and to our orthodox faith." The Greek text, while far from perfection in terms of modern criticism, represented a revolutionary achievement in that it signaled the displacement of the *Vulgata latina* from the center of biblical scholarship.

But even as early as 1514, two years before Erasmus published his edition, the illustrious Francisco Cardinal Ximénes (d. 1517) had already prepared and printed his stupendous *Complutum,* the Complutensian Polyglot—the Old Testament in Hebrew, Greek and Latin, and the New Testament in Greek and Latin. Held up for certain technical reasons, it went into circulation only in 1522. Somewhat later, in 1528, Santes Pagninus, O.P., brought out a new Latin translation of both the Old and the New Testaments which was based on the original texts; and, in the following year, Augustine Steuchus published a Latin translation of the Old Testament corrected on the basis of the Hebrew text. These few examples are only a moderate sample of the intellectual activity of the biblical scholars of this period. The whole tendency is characterized by its pronounced emphasis on the sources of the Christian religion.

But the introduction of philology into biblical studies was not universally accepted by Catholic theologians. Many of them, representatives of the old school of theology, deeply resented the intrusion of this new instrument of scholarship into theological method. In an address to the governing body of the University of Oxford St. Thomas More found it necessary to

take sharp issue with a certain 'Trojan' preacher who had in-
veighed against the Greek language from the pulpit. The saint's
discourse bristles with resentment:[43]

He (that is, the 'Trojan') says that nothing is of importance except
theology. How can he know theology if he is ignorant of Hebrew,
and Greek, and Latin? He thinks, I presume, that it can all be found
in the scholastic conundrums. Those I admit can be learned with
no particular effort. But theology, that august Queen of Heaven, demands an ampler scope. The knowledge of God can be gathered
only out of Scripture—Scripture and the early Catholic Fathers.
That was where for a thousand years the searchers after truth looked
for it and found it.

And somewhat later in a passionate defense of Erasmus he
penned a long argumentative letter of which the following few
lines are a specimen of his thinking on the then current philological problem:[44]

. . . You complain of the study of Greek and Hebrew. You say it
leads to the neglect of Latin. Was not the New Testament written
in Greek? Is truth only to be found in Gothic Latin? . . . You
pretend that the Gospels can be understood without Greek, that
there is no need of a new translation. We have the Vulgate and
others besides, you say, and a new version was superfluous. I beseech you, where are these others? I have never met a man who has
seen any but the Vulgate. Produce them. And for the Vulgate
itself, it is nonsense to talk of the many ages for which it has been
approved by the Church. It was the best or the first which the
Church could get. When once in use it could not easily be changed,
but to use it is not to approve it as perfect. . . .

The letter as a whole is a valuable witness to the desperate impatience and frustration of the enlightened Catholic on the eve of the Reformation with that exaggerated traditionalism which too often is the decisive factor in the Church's approach to problems.

Perhaps the clearest statement of the traditionalists, the adherents of the *Via antiqua,* is the *Dialogue on the Three Languages and Theological Study* composed in 1518 by Latomus of the Louvain school of theology.[45] Here we find the primacy of the Latin Vulgate and the Latin language over Hebrew and Greek exposed and defended on the basis of theological method rather than of sentimental conservatism. Perhaps the cardinal principle in Latomus' treatise is that Holy Scripture, which has been entrusted to the Church for her teaching and piety, is essentially a *doctrinal book.* The central vocation, therefore, of the theologian is to extract doctrine from it under the guidance of the Church's *magisterium.* For this special work he has no need of Hebrew and Greek, since the text of the Vulgate is obvious enough, at least so far as its theological meaning is concerned. The philologian, however, has a different orientation—to words rather than to ideas. It is his vocation to study the sacred text in Hebrew and Greek as a collection of words. As ideas are distinguished from words, so is theology from philology. The theologian is *doctus,* the philologian *eruditus.* The former is dedicated to doctrine, the latter to words.

In terms of Latomus' conception of Catholic theology various levels of opposition can be distinguished between the *old* and the *new,* between the theologian and the humanist. The former gravitates to the abstract, the idea and the doctrine; the latter to the concrete, the text and the person. For the scholastic theologian Christian life is grasped in terms of orthodoxy and morality. He looks primarily at the community and tradition. The humanist, on the other hand, sees life as an experience, a felt encounter. His gaze is intent and fixed on the individual and independence. There is question here of different mentalities which express themselves in a certain opposition (or rather differentiated centers of interest) between logic and psychology, orthodoxy and wisdom, fidelity to tradition and personal discovery. The humanist brings to theology criticism based on philology and rhetoric, while the theologian approaches it with metaphysics and dialectic. The former rests on the patristic tradition, the latter on the scholastic. The one seeks the purity of the Gospel through philology, the other doctrinal integrity through philosophy.

In the years between the publication of Latomus' *Dialogus* and the middle of the sixteenth century a Bible revolution was taking place in the Western world. In September 1522 Luther published his German translation of the New Testament, and by 1534 the entire Bible had been translated and published in German. Based on the Greek text and very probably on the Hebrew text, it became a national literary monument.[46] In a very short time the first edition of the New Testament was exhausted; and in the course of the first decade after its appearance it went through one hundred editions. No Catholic version could match the charm and vigor of its language. In 1523 Lefèvre d'Etaples (d. 1536) brought out a French translation of the New Testament; and in 1525 the unfortunate William Tyndale (d. 1536) commenced the publication of his

English version of the Bible at Cologne.[47] All the evidence
shows that these different translations made a direct appeal
to the people, were read everywhere with the utmost interest,
and left a deep and lasting impression on their readers. "The
translation of the Bible into the languages of the people had
actually become the pace maker of the Lutheran reform."
Luther rejoiced in his vast accomplishment:[48] "I thank God
that I hear and find my God in the German language in a way
in which I have not found Him up to now in the Latin, Greek
or Hebrew tongues."

Though Erasmus, as early as 1516, in the preface to his
Greek New Testament, had demanded a vernacular translation
of the Holy Scripture to make it accessible to the people, his
request was ignored by ecclesiastical authority. In view of what
the Reformers had already accomplished in this area, the need
was pressing. But despite the contemporary movement of ideas,
the Catholics of the English-speaking world would have to wait
almost seventy years for an approved English translation of
Scripture, until the appearance of the Douai version in 1582.
It is far from easy either to understand or to explain this negli-
gence in light of the precarious position of the Church in the
sixteenth century.

In the fifty years between 1512 and 1563 two ecumenical
councils, 'gathered in the Holy Spirit,' had been called to reform the Church. Neither provided for official vernacular editions of the Bible for the different linguistic groups that make
up the Western Church. The Fifth Lateran Council (1512-
1517) did not grasp the significance of the problem, while the
Council of Trent (1545-63) clearly appreciated it but offered

no solution. This was regrettable, since all the necessary re-
sources were on hand. By the beginning of the sixteenth century both the Greek and the Hebrew texts of the Bible were
available. Catholic scholars skilled in the techniques both of
language and translation were willing to put their learning
to the service of this worthy cause. Since the publication of the
Gutenberg Bible in the middle of the fifteenth century, the
printing press had become a relatively common convenience.
And the Catholic world at large wanted to read the Word of
God in the language of its life.

The solemnities of the opening of the Council of Trent took
place on December 14, 1545. Some weeks later, on February
18, 1546, Martin Luther died at Eisleben. The difficult religious
problems which he had created in the course of the past twenty-
five years, especially the burning problem of the Bible and its
relation to Christian life and thought, were to occupy a prominent place in the opening discussions of the Council. In the
various public and private sessions held between February 12th
and June 17, 1546, the Fathers of the Council devoted their
attention to the biblical problem and to other related questions:
among them, the canonicity of Scripture, its proclamation and
translation, the authenticity of the text of the *Vulgata latina,*
the relation of Scripture to the deposit of faith, tradition and
theology, and the education of clergy and laity in the Bible.
In terms of the pre-history of the Council, the Fathers could
not refuse to examine the Catholic concept of Holy Scripture
in light of the dictum *sola Scriptura,* and this posed the difficult problem of formulating their understanding of dogmatic
tradition. The task was enormous, for the biblical crisis, which

in the past fifty years had become acute, had its roots deep in the Middle Ages.[49]

Among the tasks assigned to the Fathers in preparation for the conciliar decrees on Holy Scripture was the examination of the abuses which had gradually crept into the Church's ordinary use of the Bible. At a special session held on March 1, 1546 Cardinal Marcellus Cervini, the papal legate, underlined three principal abuses for the consideration of the Fathers:[50] first, the lack of a uniform critical text of the Latin Bible, that is, a text constructed on Hebrew and Greek manuscripts; second, the lack of theologians well-versed in Sacred Scripture. And on this point the Cardinal made the telling observation:[51]

For very many, in fact almost all even of those who claim to be theologians have learned all that they know of Sacred Scripture not from the sacred books as a source, but what they learn is from the allegations of the sacred theologians whom they read; by this method not only do they poorly learn, but in their teaching others are lead into the same errors.

The third abuse which the Cardinal pointed out was the lack of preachers intellectually prepared for this office. "They do not," he said, "proclaim to the Christian people the Word of God as they should."

In commenting on the problem of the inadequate exegesis then prevalent, the bishop of Bertinoro, Thomas Casellus, O.P., reprimanded the neglect of traditional exegesis in favor of a philological one. This attitude was to be expected since the bishop's theology was based on the old medieval scholastic tradition. Thus, he said, there are "men, who vituperate in our doctors that interpretation of the divine pronouncements of Christ and Paul which has been handed down to us allegorically (as they say)."[52] But in his comprehension of the current biblical crisis he rightly saw a close connection between the proclamation of the Word of God and its study, between the task of preacher and exegete. As biblical exegesis is, so is the sacred oratory which flows from it. On the universities, the traditional center of Bible study, his observation is to the point; it links up biblical decadence with educational decadence:[53]

Now I come to abuses in the universities, which, though they have received from the supreme pontiff and the councils the power of naming masters, doctors, bachelors and preachers, so abuse this authority that for human favor and pecuniary gain they constitute and elevate unlearned men (I will not say ignoramuses) to these grades, and this happens not without the greatest shame and hurt to the Christian religion. And I am speaking here of apostolic legates, of counts of the empire, of prothonotaries who, as I have said above, abuse this power which they have.

Then Girolamo Seripando (d. 1563), the General of the Augustinian Hermits, rose to present his understanding of the misuse of Scripture in the Church:[54]

Preaching, he said, should be ordered to salvation. Therefore, let those who want to teach Holy Scripture first learn it well that they might teach it well. [In their sermons, preachers] should not discuss speculative questions but the real sacred letters; and, they should teach the youth a Christian doctrine which is not excerpted from philosophy, but they should interpret Sacred Scripture from Sacred Scripture according to Paul and Augustine.

This insistence on biblical study, preaching and catechesis reveals clearly the humanistic tendencies of Seripando. "When he spoke, thus, he countered without naming him, the attack made by the bishop of Bertinoro . . . on the philological and literal interpretation of Holy Scripture."[55]

But perhaps of all the Fathers it was Thomas Campeggio, the bishop of Feltre, whose remarks on the question of biblical versions were most adamant and progressive:[56]

I do not think, he said, that it should be regarded as an abuse, that the sacred books are read in the vernacular, for St. Jerome published a translation of the Mass in the Illyrian language, and its use was permitted by the Church of Illyria . . . I do think that the Ordinaries should use the utmost effort to see that the sacred books be translated faithfully into the common language [of the people]. . . .

Campeggio's plea, out of harmony with the age's ecclesiastical thought and practice, went unheeded.[57]

On March 4th the decision was made by the Fathers to form a committee which would prepare a general list of the biblical abuses for consideration by a future general congregation of the Council. This special group, composed of both bishops and theologians, was to sift and weigh the proposals which had been made by the Fathers, to hear the *pros* and *cons* of each question, and, on the basis of all this information, to prepare a report for definitive action.[58] On March 9th the Fathers in special session listened "with wondrous attention" as Alfonso De Castro, O.F.M., discoursed on the question of vernacular versions of the Bible. The negative tenor of his thought is almost unbelievable. "The parent and origin of heresies is the translation of Sacred Scripture into the vernacular. For thus it happens that it is read by men without any distinction of persons."[59] Then the old argument is produced once again. If learned men cannot understand Scripture, how can unlearned? They cannot, of course! Even history shows that sacred books should not be read by all. Thus, in olden times the reading of the Sibylline books was restricted to only ten men. "How much more fitting is it, therefore, that Christians show such reverence to Scripture that it be not given over to be read by every Tom, Dick and Harry." In this vein he continues on, rejecting with every conceivable argument the dissemination of the Bible in the mother tongue.[60]

It is not surprising, therefore, that the report which the committee submitted on March 17th simply omitted from conciliar decision the question of vernacular translations of Scripture. We are grateful at least that Trent did not condemn the preparation of popular versions of the Bible, if it did not approve it. When the list of abuses was read in the general congregation the Spanish cardinal Pacheco, far from being satisfied with the Council's official silence on this point, was extremely irritated that the preparation of vernacular versions of Scripture was not listed among the biblical abuses and, therefore, as a source of scandal to the Church.[61] At this point the Prince-Bishop of Trent, Cristoforo Madruzzo, rose to refute his Spanish colleague:[62]

I would not want, if I could help it, to oppose the sentiments of my most Reverend Lord of Jaen. But in view of the freedom of speech

which God has given us, I am forced to say these things which seem
to me so true that they cannot be hidden. I want to make this
point, that we should never tolerate the vernacular version of the
Scripture to be enumerated among abuses. What indeed would
our adversaries say to the people to whom they are daily preaching
idle things, if they were to learn that we wish to snatch from the
hands of men the Holy Scripture which blessed Paul the apostle
thought should never be separated from our mouth. From experience
I know that the Lord's Prayer and the Creed and many other
things were communicated to me in our German tongue. These
and other prayers every father of a family throughout all Germany is accustomed to teach his little ones. And from this kind of
education never within the memory of man has scandal come. . . .

To Cardinal Pacheco's retort that he did not mean 'abuse,'
but that he did know that prohibitory laws had been passed in
Spain about this matter and that Pope Paul II had confirmed
them, Madruzzo replied in burning words:[63]

Pope Paul and all the popes at times can and could err. (I do not
say that they have.) But the Gospel of Paul the Apostle, who
wished that the Gospel of Christ never be removed from our
mouth, could not err. And so I say, in this matter there should be
no controversy.

Pacheco remained adamant in his conviction that the vernacular Bibles were a biblical abuse and should be recognized
as such by the Council. And this principle he maintained,
notwithstanding the fact that in a private interview on March
22nd the secretary of the Council, Massarelli, had explained

to him among other things that there were whole nations, Germany and Poland for example, which would not accept a conciliar decree outlawing the reading of the Bible in the mother tongue. But well aware of the stern prohibitions which their Catholic Majesties, Ferdinand and Isabella, had directed against this 'abuse' in their realms. Pacheco adhered to his position.[64]

While the anti-vernacular block (Spain and Italy) did not fully triumph in the Council, it did make its influence felt, at least negatively.[65] Thus, in the Fourth Session on April 8th the Council promulgated a solemn decree on many of the biblical problems, but it neither condemned nor approved the preparation of vernacular editions of Scripture. By its studied silence in this compelling matter, it left the burden to the individual bishops of the Church, if they cared to assume it. This was unfortunate. One official sentence in favor of a vernacular version of Scripture and its common use by the faithful would have meant so very much for the piety, doctrine and worship of the Church. In effect, the Council's refusal to act retarded certain lines of Catholic spiritual development for centuries.

In the late spring of 1546, after the fourth session, the Fathers turned their attention to the place of the Word of God in Christian life, above all to its communication to the people. This question involved the reformation of preaching—a problem complex in its own right and further complicated because it involved other issues of massive importance: for example, the perennial contest between the regulars and the seculars, and the delicate relation of the 'new' to the 'old' learning. This debate on the reform of preaching was calculated to call into question personal values and vested interests. In probing the validity of old traditions it trod on highly sensitive areas.

Long before the middle of the sixteenth century the office of preaching had passed by default from the diocesan clergy to the mendicant friars. Clerical education in the course of the centuries had decayed, and in consequence qualified preachers were rare among the diocesan clergy. But the transference of the office of preaching to the mendicants made for a certain lopsidedness in the external structure of the Church. The bishops, incapable of or disinterested in the pulpit, had *de facto* to rely on the mendicants for whatever preaching would be heard in their dioceses. And the mendicants in the course of the centuries had acquired through papal exemption a certain independence of episcopal control which did not always make for efficient diocesan government. All this was further complicated by the fact that the mendicants could not always be relied upon for good conduct, sound doctrine and general prudence.[66]

The reformation of preaching involved the reform of clerical education, which was to be orientated to a fundamentally biblical theology. This was to be done in the hope that thereby the ministry of the Word would be reformed, and that this renewal would lead to a reformation of the spiritual life of the faithful. The approach was indirect: biblical education of the laity through biblical education of the clergy. But the problem of theological education, when it was raised at Trent, sharply divided and deadlocked the Fathers in terms of their commitment to humanism or scholasticism. The sharp exchange in the general congregation of May 20th between Don Isidoro, the abbot of Pontida, and Domingo Soto, O.P., the imperial theologian, brings out the character of these two different concepts of the primacy of the Bible in clerical education.[67]

In the fifth session on June 17, 1546 a reform decree was passed on "the establishment of lectureships in Holy Scripture and the liberal arts." This decree, which provided for clerical education in "reading and preaching" the Bible, has been rightly described as "the only successful attempt to combine Church reform with whatever was sound in Christian humanism."[68] But its influence did not reach far.

The humanism of the early sessions of Trent yielded to a revitalized scholasticism in the later phases of the Council. Thus the priest-seminaries[69] which the Fathers decreed (can. 18) in the twenty-third session on July 15, 1563, developed more under the scholastic influence than the humanistic. Guided more by traditional than progressive considerations, the architects of these new schools sought inspiration in the distant past, as far back perhaps as the monastic schools of the Carolingian Renaissance. In view of the formative elements of this new clerical education, its subsequent development is normal. Thus the urban faculties of theology were gradually deserted, for in the post-Tridentine ideal the priest was to be educated in a private seminary rather than at a public university. His priestly training was more moral than intellectual. Ultimately the seminary would move to quiet, pastoral scenes where, secluded from the affairs of men, the seminarians would lead a life disciplined about prayer and study. And though this seclusion from the world distorted the practical, pastoral aspects of their training, it remains almost connatural to sacerdotal education. Obviously the traditionalism which inspired this kind of clerical formation did not have in it the creative elements which could give the Church that biblical and liturgical reformation which she needed.

This chapter has described in broad outline the Bible legacy which the Tridentine age received from the Middle Ages and which in turn it has transmitted to us. In many respects, both intellectual and pastoral, the modern Church is deeply concerned with the solution of this inherited problem. One of the most concrete expressions of her attempt to transcend the past five hundred years of her history and to repossess the rich biblical tradition of the ancient Church is the *Constitution on the Sacred Liturgy* (II, 51) of December 4, 1963. The Council declares here:

The treasures of the Bible are to be opened up more lavishly so that richer fare may be provided for the faithful at the table of the Word of God.

These words are worthy of the best aspects of the patristic tradition, for they underline the Church's intention that Scripture be fundamental to Catholic life.[70]

But in planning this true reformation of the spiritual life of the faithful, the Church is also aware that the education of her priests must be renewed and revitalized. The methods of the past have outlived their usefulness. The Tridentine heritage— the seminary system—is exhausted. One seeks neither a new dogmatic teaching nor a new priesthood, but a new theological expression of dogma and a new approach to the formation of priests. For, as the official witness of the Church, the priest must be intellectually and spiritually prepared to represent her to the world as she is. He must know not only the formulas of Word and Sacrament but also their meaning; and in terms of the day and age in which he lives, it is his vocation to communicate this saving message to the contemporary world.

NOTES

[1] John 1:17.

[2] This is especially significant when one considers that from the Patristic period down to the end of the Middle Ages theology and exegesis coincided. Cf. H. DeLubac, S.J., *Exégèse médiévale* 1, 1 (Paris 1959), pp. 59–74.

[3] Cf. L. Bouyer, "Les psaumes et la catéchèse chrétienne," *Maison-Dieu* 33 (1953), pp. 8–20, and B. Fischer, "Le Christ dans les Psaumes," *ibid.*, pp. 86–109.

[4] St. Augustine in his *De catechizandis rudibus* 3, 1 holds the view that catechesis should commence with the text, "In the beginning God created heaven and earth," and continue down to the present days of the Church. He seems to have envisioned both Bible and Church History as integral parts of catechetical instruction. In his *De doctrina christiana* 1, 21–39; 40, he teaches that the reading of Scripture is ordered to love of God and man. Cf. R. M. Grant, "The Bible in the Ancient Church," *Journal of Religion* 26 (1946), pp. 199–200.

[5] For example, St. Jerome (d. 420) undertook the preparation of the *Vulgata latina* as a vernacular translation under the auspices of Pope Damasus I (d. 384). This was to be the last great biblical undertaking of the papacy until the unfortunate edition (1590) of the Vulgate under Sixtus V.

[6] This is the conclusion of Homily 16 on the book of Numbers. Cf. A. Hamman, ed., *Early Christian Prayers* (Chicago 1961), p. 41.

[7] Cf. C. Mirbt, *Quellen zur Geschichte des Papsttums und des römischen Katholizismus,* no. 210, p. 98.

[8] J. Jungmann, S.J., *The Good News Yesterday and Today* trans. by W. A. Huesman, S.J. (New York 1962), p. 24.

[9] For example, St. Ambrose's *Commentary on St. Luke,* and St. Augustine's *Commentary on St. John.*

[10] Cf. H. DeLubac, S.J., *op. cit.*, p. 60: For example, "in the language of St. Gregory the Great, the *divinae doctrinae eruditio* was the teaching given by the Scripture, and the saintly pope conceived of no other 'theology' save that which consists in *sacri eloquii erudiri mysteriis*."

[11] Note St. Augustine's (*De catechizandis rudibus* 4, 8) expression of this theme: "In veteri testamento est occultatio novi, in novo testamento est manifestatio veteris."

[12] Cf. J. Quasten, "The Painting of the Good Shepherd at Dura-Europas," *Mediaeval Studies* 9 (1947), pp. 1–18.

[13] *Adversus Haereses* 3, 6, 4. Cf. A. Hamman, *op. cit.*, pp. 30–31, and n. 1.

[14] *Historia ecclesiastica* 8, 2, 4. Cf. B. J. Kidd, *Documents Illustrative of the History of the Church*, Vol. 1 no. 185, p. 238.

[15] *De morte persecutorum* 12, 2. Cf. B. J. Kidd, *ibid*. no. 180, p. 232.

[16] J. Stevenson, *A New Eusebius*, no. 249, p. 288.

[17] Cf. F. Schneider, *Rom und Romgedanke im Mittelalter* (Munich 1926), p. 5: "According to a medieval proverb the monopoly of the three great nations was divided in this way: Germany had *Imperium*, Italy *Sacerdotium*, France *Studium*. Thus one can say of Rome that it had thrice ruled the world, in antiquity through *Imperium*, in the Middle Ages through *Sacerdotium*, in modern times through *Studium*."

[18] In this regard the words of Cardinal Allen are highly significant: "Catholics educated in the academies and schools have hardly any knowledge of the Scriptures except in Latin. When they are preaching to the unlearned and are obliged on the spur of the moment to translate some passage into the vernacular, they often do it inaccurately. . . ." Cf. H. Pope, O.P., *English Versions of the Bible* (London 1952), p. 250.

[19] "Mira profunditas," writes St. Augustine, "eloquiorum tuorum . . . Mira profunditas, Deus meus, mira profunditas!" *Confessions* 12, 14, 17.

[20] *The Dialogue Concerning Tyndale*, 3, 16, W. E. Campbell, ed. (London 1927), p. 243.

[21] For example, the Latin Bible in St. Gall (Stiftsbibliothek, Cod. 75) contains 418 parchment folios numbered from 1 to 840. It was prepared at Tours, about 801–804, probably under Alcuin and measures 22"x16". Cf. B. Fischer, O.S.B., *Die Alkuin-Bibel* (Freiburg 1957), p. 10.

[22] Cf. his *Gemma ecclesiastica* 2, 341 where we read: "There is the case of the priest who was preaching to the people a sermon about St. Barnabas, and he said among other things: 'He was a good man and a saint, but he used, however, to be a robber.' For his authority was that verse of the Gospel, namely, 'Now Barabbas was a robber,' and he did not properly distinguish

between Barnabas and Barabbas. . . ." These and other amusing examples cited by M. Deanesly, *The Lollard Bible* (Cambridge 1920), pp. 194–95, though significant, are not wholly typical.

23 Cf. C. Mirbt, *op. cit.*, no 320, p. 173; M. Deanesly, *op. cit.*, pp. 30–35; and H. Grundmann, *Religiöse Bewegungen im Mittelalter* (Hildesheim 1961), pp. 97–100.

24 Cf. C. Mirbt, *op. cit.*, nos. 321–22, p. 174.

25 Pope Innocent's letter, *Cum ex coniuncto*, passed into the *Decretals* of Gregory IX and so into the universal canon law. At the Reformation it was cited as a decree forbidding vernacular translations of Scripture, which actually it did not.

26 Before the appearance of Luther's translation in 1522 there were at least fourteen published German versions of the Bible in existence.

27 Cf. C. Mirbt, *op. cit.*, no. 352, p. 194.

28 Cf. on the history and historical background of this Bible M. Deanesly's work cited above.

29 It was condemned in 1408 by a synod at Oxford under Archbishop Arundel: "We establish and order that henceforth no one on his own authority shall translate any text of the Holy Scripture into the English language. . . ." The 'saving' phrase is "on his own authority"; but the point is that no ecclesiastical authority lent weight to the making of an English version.

30 Outstanding exceptions are John Scotus Erigena in the early Middle Ages who knew Greek quite perfectly, and Nicholas of Lyra in the late Middle Ages who had mastered Hebrew.

31 Cf. B. Smalley, *The Study of the Bible in the Middle Ages* (Oxford 1952), and R. E. McNally, S.J., *The Bible in the Early Middle Ages,* Woodstock Papers 4 (Westminster 1959).

32 Cf. H. DeLubac, S.J., *op. cit.*, 1, 1, pp. 94 ff.

33 Exceptional here was Nicholas of Lyra (d. 1340) who wrote: "The writings of the Fathers are not of such great authority that no one is allowed to think in a contrary sense in those matters which have not been determined by Sacred Scripture itself."

34 Cf. H. DeLubac, S.J., *op. cit.*, 1, 1, pp. 221 ff.

35 *Summa gloria* 1, 2, *Libelli de lite* 3 (Hannover 1897) p. 65.

36 Of the four senses of Scripture Luther wrote: "With these trifling and foolish fables they [the idle and unlearned monks and the school doctors] rent the Scriptures into so many and diverse senses that silly poor consciences could receive no doctrine at all." Cf. L. W. Spitz, *The Religious Renaissance of the German Humanists* (Cambridge, Mass. 1963), p. 255.

[37] *The Praise of Folly* [28], trans. by H. H. Hudson (Princeton 1951), pp. 77–78.

[38] *Ibid.*, [31], pp. 91–2.

[39] H. J. Grimm, ed., *Career of the Reformer* 1, *Luther's Works* 31 (Philadelphia 1957), p. 12.

[40] *Against Latomus*, tr., G. Lindbeck, *Career of the Reformer* 2, *Luther's Works* 32 (Philadelphia 1958), pp. 257–58.

[41] *Ibid.*, p. 259. In his *Address to the German Nobility* Luther protested "against the practice that allows a mere bachelor at the university to lecture on the Bible, while the *Sentences* of the Lombard can be interpreted only by a doctor of theology and a priest." Cf. R. Fife, *The Revolt of Martin Luther* (New York 1957), pp. 517–18.

[42] Cf. L. W. Spitz, *op. cit.*, p. 199.

[43] J. A. Froude, *Life and Letters of Erasmus* (New York 1927), p. 141.

[44] *Ibid.*, p. 145.

[45] Cf. R. Guelluy, "L'evolution des methodes théologiques à Louvain d'Erasme à Jansenius," *Revue d'histoire ecclesiastique* 37 (1941), pp. 31–144, to which I am especially indebted for the development of these pages.

[46] Cf. on Luther's 'inspirational view' of the Bible, W. Schwarz, *Principles and Problems of Biblical Translation* (Cambridge 1955), pp. 167–212.

[47] In the autumn of 1535 he was arrested near Brussels, imprisoned, strangled and burnt at the stake.

[48] Cited by L. W. Spitz, *op. cit.*, p. 241, from Luther's preface to the *Theologia Deutsch* (1518).

[49] Cf. H. Jedin, *A History of the Council of Trent*, Vol. 2 (St. Louis 1958), pp. 67 ff.

[50] *A. Massarelli Diarium* III, S. Merkle, ed., *Concilium Tridentinum* 1, 1 (Freiburg 1901), p. 506.

[51] *Ibid.*

[52] *Ibid.*, p. 505.

[53] *Ibid.*

[54] *Ibid.*

[55] H. Jedin, *op. cit.*, Vol. 2, p. 69.

[56] *A. Massarelli Diarium* III, *Concilium Tridentinum* 1, 1, 503. Actually the evidence is against St. Jerome's authorship of an Illyrian translation of the Missal. But the point is that the bishop was trying to formulate an argument from the practice of Christian antiquity against the 'traditionalists' in the Council. Cf. *Ibid.*, Vol. 1, p. 503, n. 3.

[57] For example, Coriolano Martirano, bishop of San Marco, considered the

publishing of the sacred books in the vernacular to be a most grave abuse; and Giacomo Giacomelli, bishop of Belcastro, argued that in no manner should permission be given for the translation of Scripture. Cf. *Ibid.*, 504.

[58] The three theologians appointed to this committe as *periti* were the Frenchman Richard of Le Mans, the Spaniard Alfonso De Castro and the Italian Ambrosius Catharinus. The two latter had written learned treatises against vernacular versions of the Bible.

[59] A. De Castro, *Adversus Haereses* 1, 13 (Venice 1546), pp. 143 ff.

[60] He was, for example, particularly disturbed by current erroneous private interpretations of Scripture. "What is worst of all," he writes, "this is done not only by men but also by women. Paul certainly did not allow women to teach. Nevertheless, in these days with Luther's favor women are not afraid to teach and dispute about the faith, and so imprudently that you can more easily win back a hundred men from error than one woman." Cf. A. De Castro, *op. cit.*, p. 148.

[61] Cf. H. Severolus, *Commentarius,* ed., S. Merkle, *Concilium Tridentinum* 1, 1, p. 37.

[62] *Ibid.*

[63] *Ibid.*, p. 38.

[64] Cf. on this prohibition of the Spanish monarchy F. H. Reusch, *Der Index der verbotenen Bücher,* Vol. 1 (Bonn 1883) p. 44. A. De Castro, Pacheco's theologian, referred to this law as the "laudandum . . . edictum." Cf. A. De Castro, *op. cit.*, p. 144.

[65] The anti-vernacularists were not totally opposed to the laity's reading Scripture. Thus, Pacheco was willing to allow them to read Proverbs, Acts, Psalms and the like; but under no circumstances should the Apocalypse, the epistles of Paul, especially to the Romans, Ezechiel, and books of this kind be allowed to fall into the hands of "the common people, rustics and women." Cf. A. Massarelli, *Diarium* III *Concilium Tridentinum* 1, 1, p. 520.

[66] Cf. H. Jedin, *op. cit.*, Vol. 2, pp. 101 ff.

[67] *Ibid.*

[68] *Ibid.*, p. 122.

[69] The word, *seminarium,* meaning 'a nursery, a nursery-garden, a seed-plot,' is instructive. It suggests a special place wherein fragile, delicate, tender young men are secluded for special cultivation.

[70] Equally important, but from the intellectual aspect, is the great biblical encyclical of Pius XII, *Divino afflante Spiritu.*

4 * Liturgy

IT IS THE PROPER TASK of the Church to lead men to faith in Christ and through Him to union with God. Through Christ, the great celestial mediator, the Church dispenses generously to all men His "grace and truth," because to her Word and Sacrament[1] the summit and the core of the Christian life have been entrusted. The Word, the new *evangelium,* the saving message of salvation to all men of all times, is God's revelation through Christ the Lord, His only Son. The Sacrament, the Christian mystery, is font of life, source of grace, light of the spirit. Including in its broadest sense both the sacrifice of the Mass and the Eucharist, it is the medium through which Christ acts *on* and *with* the faithful. Sacrament involves mystical elevation and deification by grace, and a wondrous transformation of the children of men into sons of God. On earth the Church, Christ's Mystical Body, is the Lord's efficacious instrument for accomplishing these lofty purposes of Word and

Sacrament. It is as minister of "grace and truth" that she fulfills her role in salvation history.

Through grace the Church unites man with God. Through worship, through the liturgy as the common action of the whole Christian community gathered about the altar, she dispenses grace to all. Because the victim which the people of God offer in sacrifice is so spotless, acceptable and venerable, their reverent prayer is heard. God's grace descends with power to strengthen and to maintain their supernatural life, to gather them together into close union in His Mystical Body.

The liturgy of the Church is ancient in origin. It reaches back to the Supper Room where Christ, surrounded by His Apostles, sat down to His last Paschal feast on the night before He died. In a highly religious setting, vividly recalling and reproducing God's ancient covenant with His people in the Old Testament, Christ offered Himself as a new victim in a new sacrifice. He inaugurated in fact a new testament, a new order of things, a new kingdom of God on earth in which sin and error would yield to "grace and truth." Under the meaningful symbols of bread and wine Christ presented His Body and Blood as a sacrificial offering for the remission of sin, the redemption of the world, the destruction of death. What Christ did *then*, the Church does *now*. By endless repetition of the solemn action of the Supper Room her priesthood shows forth forever "the death of the Lord until He come again." While the Last Supper looked forward to the immolation of Calvary which it anticipated, the Mass looks back to it as the foundation of its fullness, the ultimate cause of its existence, the true guarantee of its efficacy.

Historically and theologically the liturgy is rooted in the Supper Room.[2] By the will of Christ His priests reproduce over and over again this central event in salvation history and apply its fruits to mankind. In the primitive Church public worship was simple in form. Inspired fundamentally by the Lord's action in the Supper Room, though structured more closely on the *chaburah,* the Jewish Sabbath meal, it was biblical, sacrificial, communal, ecclesial and commemorative in character. It included singing of hymns, reading of Scripture, pastoral homily, ritualistic offering and communal communion of the faithful. The rite embraced elements both of sacrifice and banquet. For the Victim which was offered by the Church to God the Father was shared by His people as a worshipping community. United in "the communion of the breaking of the bread and in the prayers," priest and people worshipped together. This assembly was "of one heart and one soul." It is this Eucharistic unity which St. Ignatius of Antioch (d. *ca.* 107) warmly recommends in his letter to the Philadelphians:[3]

Take care, then, to partake of one Eucharist. For one is the Flesh of our Lord Jesus Christ, and one the cup to unite us with His Blood, and one altar, just as there is one bishop assisted by the presbytery and the deacons, my fellow servants. Thus you will conform in all your actions to the will of God.

In the fifteen centuries which separate the Last Supper from the first evangelical Lord's Supper (1521), the primitive rite of the Mass developed in different directions, linguistic, rubrical, structural and textual. Without forsaking its essential elements

as 'a memorial to the Lord,' it yielded to the climate of contemporary culture; it accomodated itself to the needs of the
different national groups of the faithful as the Church of the
first centuries spread throughout and beyond the civilized
world. Thus an Eastern (Oriental) and a Western (Latin) rite
emerged; and in the West, especially during the opening years
of the Middle Ages, the old Mass rite was more and more
adapted to particular usage and observance which in time gave
rise to national, and even local rites. This genetic process was
not extraordinary, for the historical Church is subject to the
laws of growth; and in these early times, when personal initiative enjoyed considerable freedom, growth was inevitable. The
diversity of prayer forms and liturgical practice which crept
into the order of divine worship was largely conditioned and
determined by the important consideration that the membership of the early medieval Church in the West represented a
mélange of peoples, Latin, Gothic, Celtic and Germanic, each
creative in terms of its own national culture and local environ-
ment.

These accretions to the primitive Mass rites did not themselves create a problem, for as simple accumulations they could
have been eliminated by simple severance, if uniformity had
been desirable. Our concern is not with the origin of rites; it is
rather with the devious mutations in liturgical worship which
in the course of time almost succeeded in extinguishing it. For
the transformation of worship between the end of Late Antiquity and the end of the Middle Ages involved and expressed
a profound change in the religious mentality of the faithful,
in their approach to divine things, in their understanding of

Word and Sacrament. Exposed to a variety of cultural and theological influences, the liturgical sense of the people gradually became distorted. Over the centuries Catholic worship drifted slowly, imperceptibly, away from its primitive spirit which was simple, objective and corporate, to an undisciplined state of flamboyancy, subjectivism and personalism. In the dark shadows so characteristic of the autumn time of medieval culture it is hard to recognize in Catholic liturgy the pure elements of the ancient Christian worship from which it had sprung. For though the true sense of worship—lost in a maze of extraneous detail accumulated over the centuries—was indeed present in the Church as Christ's institution, it was not appreciated. The minds of the responsible ecclesiastics of that day, almost without exception, were too distracted in other directions to grasp the significance of the disaster which was evolving in this important facet of her religious life.[4]

The import of the problem can be measured from this consideration: within a few years after the close of the fifteenth century, the reformers, many of them Catholic priests and all of them born and reared in the Catholic Church, were using all means within their power to stamp out every vestige of the Mass, the most sacred, venerable act of worship in the Catholic religion. Why did these men, who had grown up in an atmosphere in which the Mass was paramount, turn against their ancient heritage? Why did they forsake in the name of Christian reform the old ways of worship to find new ones? These delicate questions are raised here neither to excuse the reformers nor to place them in a more favorable light, but rather to help uncover some of the basic, fundamental motives of the reformation whose effects remain to this day so deep a concern for the Church. The character of religion is expressed most concretely in its divine worship. The attitude of two of the outstanding reformers of the pre-Tridentine period to Catholic liturgy is indicative: Martin Luther was hostile, Ignatius Loyola reserved.

In one of the most brilliant essays ever written on a single point of liturgical history,[5] Josef Jungmann, S.J., has presented a highly relevant analysis of the development of Catholic worship in the years between Late Antiquity and the high Middle Ages. "No period," he writes, "has ever seen a greater revolution in religious thought and institutions than that which took place in the five centuries between the close of the patristic age and the dawn of scholasticism . . . Within the limits marked out by dogma there were taking place unobtrusively certain shifts of accent and changes of viewpoint having consequences so wide that they have left their mark on all subsequent ages right down to our own times."[6] In this distant past that pattern took shape according to which Catholic worship was to develop in the centuries leading to the Reformation and even beyond it to our own day.[7]

Formed in the opening decades of the early Middle Ages when Western civilization had almost lost the thread of continuity with the past, the medieval liturgy represented a sharp deviation from the wholesome spirit of primitive Christianity, its piety and worship, toward a stark individualism, subjectivism and personalism. The picture of worship on the eve of the Reformation is out of focus in comparison with its primitive prototype. The sharp, clear lines of the early period are blurred either in too much shadow or too much light. Here was an area of Catholic life in acute need of fundamental reformation and restoration.[8] Its neglect helped to set off explosive forces which rent Christianity in segments. It is now more than four hundred years since the faithful of Western Christendom have gathered in common faith about one recognized altar of worship.

The Catholic liturgy, as celebrated in Rome in the apostolic age, was in the Greek language, which was then the common tongue of the Mediterranean world. By the middle of the fourth century, perhaps even somewhat earlier, Latin as a liturgical language replaced Greek, which had ceased to be the everyday medium of expression in Rome. The linguistic transition was natural and agreeable to the primitive Christian mentality. Because in the liturgical action of the primitive Church priest and laity were united in common dialogue, it was considered *de rigueur* that the language of prayer should be the language of life. The communal method which the Roman Church employed in its liturgy at this early period is vividly suggested by a well-known passage in one of the oldest extant ecclesiastical ordinances, *The Apostolic Tradition* (*ca.* 200) of St. Hippolytus of Rome:[9]

To [the newly consecrated bishop] let the deacons bring the oblation and he with all the presbyters laying his hand on the oblation shall say giving thanks:
"The Lord be with you."
And the people shall say:
"And with thy spirit."

And the bishop shall say:
"Lift up your hearts."
And the people shall say:
"We have them with the Lord."
And the bishop shall say:
"Let us give thanks unto the Lord."
And the people shall say:
"It is meet and right."

There follows, then, the eucharistic prayer of thanksgiving in the name of the whole Christian community offered through the "Beloved Child Jesus Christ through whom glory and honor" is to the Father "with the Holy Spirit . . . now and forever and world without end."

The picture which St. Hippolytus presents here and in other passages of his work is not extraordinary. Other early Christian source material yields the same conclusion. In the liturgical practice of the primitive Church, priest and laity, united about the altar of sacrifice, engaged in meaningful dialogue, because the words and concepts of their prayer were readily comprehensible to both. The mystery was sought rather in the meaning of the sacred action than in the unintelligibility of the liturgical text.

By the ninth century, especially in the northern Europe of the Frankish Empire, Latin had almost ceased to be a living language as far as the majority of the people were concerned. The ordinary Christian, because he did not enjoy the benefits of formal education, knew no Latin. He thought in and spoke his own native tongue, Germanic, Romance or Celtic, and he had very little to do with Latin which was for him a bookish,

scholarly and clerical language, the special medium of the
learned world, the world of the educated clergy. But even
though the clergy itself was not always full master of its special
tongue, Latin continued to be the official prayer language of
all public worship.[10] Through constant use in the liturgy
for more than four hundred years, it had become fixed in the
tradition of the Western Church. And the special appeal that the
traditional and the archaic make in religious matters, above
all where there is question of cult, was of considerable importance in the retention of this ancient language long after it had
died.[11] To suppose that Latin was unappreciated in the early
Middle Ages would be to misread the character of medieval
culture. It was highly esteemed by clergy and laity as the
linguistic foundation of Roman civilization and culture. For
together with Hebrew and Greek it formed a classical triad of
sacred languages—sacred because both in the Bible and in the
suprascription of the Cross these languages in preference to all
others had been employed.[12] Further, the barbarian peoples of
these northern lands were keenly aware that Latin was the
language of the revered Roman Empire; part and parcel, therefore, of a venerable and treasured heritage.[13]

But there is another aspect of the retention of Latin in the
liturgy which illustrates the religious mentality of the medieval
Church. For the strict adherence to Latin was inspired neither
by tyranny nor by clericalism. The very text of the Mass, like
that of Holy Scripture, was regarded as sacred in character; it
had, therefore, to be carefully guarded from the profanation
which was thought would arise from a vernacular translation
accessible to all. Latin protected and shielded the Mass text

with a mystical and mysterious atmosphere that also served to enhance its sacral dignity. The fact that the simple laity did not understand the Latin words in which the priest prayed in their name was not considered of great importance. The medieval liturgy, orientated towards God through the clergy, prescinded from His people. The unexpressed presupposition was that the priest understood Latin; if he did not, the Lord certainly did, and that sufficed.

The history of the Canon of the Mass pointedly illustrates the tendency which is in question here.[14] Up to the fourth century the Canon seems certainly to have been said or sung by the priest in an audible tone and in a language which the people could readily comprehend. By the ninth century it had become a book virtually locked with double seals—by the silence of tone and by the mystery of language. It had become a sacerdotal prayer, a kind of sanctuary, a tabernacle or Holy of Holies into which the priest alone entered and there alone prayed his prayers in silence.[15] At a later date the violation of the Canon-silence was regarded as a grave moral evil.[16] Gradually a *schola cantorum* assumed the laity's part in the Eucharistic dialogue. It sang the *Sanctus,* for example, while silence fell on the congregation, now left to its private devotions. The priest prayed his prayers, the laity theirs. The liturgical link of community between the two was broken.

Thus the people were excluded from active participation in the great Eucharistic prayer. They did not understand Latin; they could not hear it, even if they could have understood it. There were no translations made under official auspices, while privately circulated versions were looked upon with the utmost suspicion and disfavor.[17] But no official action was taken to provide the laity and the clergy with an approved vernacular rendition of the sacred liturgical text. This obscurantist mentality long survived both the Middle Ages and the Reformation.[18] A brief (*Ad aures nostras,* January 12, 1661) of Alexander VII, with strong words of condemnation for a French translation of the Roman Missal, illustrates the continuance of this mode of thinking into the middle of the seventeenth century:[19]

We have learned with great sorrow that in the kingdom of France certain sons of perdition, itching with novelties detrimental to souls, and despising the laws and practice of the Church, have lately come to such madness as to dare to translate the Roman Missal . . . into French . . . and to hand it over to persons of every rank and sex. Thus they have attempted by their rash action to degrade the most sacred rites, to lower the majesty which the Latin language gives to them, and to expose the divine mysteries to the common gaze. . . .

In view of this official *modus videndi* it is understandable that in the liturgical wilderness of the Baroque period the important connection between the sacred text of the Mass and the sanctification of the faithful was overlooked.[20]

Within primitive Christianity the altar enjoyed a prominent place in the structure of both theology and church. At once sacrificial center and banquet table, it was situated close to the people. Frequently it was orientated 'in expectation of the Lord' and, at times, elevated and appointed in such wise that the priest and the people who gathered at "the Lord's Supper"

(1 Cor. 11:20) faced one another in a communal attitude. At other times priest and people looked together towards the East, with the priest in the prominent position of leader of the whole assembly. No single pattern is discernible in the usage of the ancient Church.[21]

The altar was simple in structure, almost cubic in dimensions, table-like (the Lord's table) in form, without tabernacle, candles or reredos, even without crucifix, since the Eucharist in itself was the adequate memorial of the Lord's death. It was the sacred table on which the Church offered to the heavenly Father her sacrifice in the name of Christ the Redeemer, and from which the faithful were fed with the new heavenly manna unto life eternal. In each church there was but one altar because of the oneness of Christ whom it mystically symbolized;[22] and about this altar the people gathered as a chosen body, as a believing community sharing in one, solemn Eucharistic action. The ritualistic offering was made in common: "Receive, O holy Father, this oblation which *we* offer. . . ." The Christian assembly which came together on the Lord's Day, the Day of the Resurrection, had an intimacy, an expectancy and an urgency about it that underlined the high significance of the Eucharist in the ethos of the early Church and reveals to us much about her inner liturgical life and religious thought.

Characteristic of the development of worship in the Middle Ages is the gradual, almost total separation of the altar from the people, and the people from the priest. The great Gothic cathedrals which arose in northern France in the course of the late twelfth and thirteenth centuries illustrate this trend. For here the altar is withdrawn into the sanctuary, almost to the back of the apse, at the greatest possible distance from the nave where the people gathered for divine services. In solitary silence, in deep shadows, in clerical aloofness, the sacred rite as a pageant unfolded beneath the splendid rose windows and the massive vaulting. Only occasionally was the silence broken by the voice of the priest; and the words which he addressed to his people were taken up and answered by the *schola cantorum* which had usurped the role of the faithful in maintaining the Eucharistic dialogue with the priest.

The late medieval development of Gothic architecture further confirmed the trends which had been developing over the centuries past. The altar was increasingly absorbed by the imposing sanctuary; in blending with this vast structure it came more and more to lose its primitive character as table of sacrifice, and developed more as a work of art than as the center of cult. Ultimately it became simply an appendage to the lofty reredos. At times an ornate screen was erected between nave and apse so that the seclusion of the sanctuary and the altar of sacrifice was total.[23]

The artistic representation of the crucifix, which first appeared on the altar in the course of the ninth century, also experienced a striking transformation. Its primitive design as a symbol of that *beata passio* in which Christ came to the fullness of victory was gradually displaced. Thus the crucified King of Glory of the Romanesque period yielded to the crucified Suffering Servant of the late Middle Ages; a period marked by stark realism and pronounced sentimentality, with an emphasis on Calvary as a tragic stage on which the Lord of life was overwhelmed by ignominy, outrage and suffering, the high price which His redeeming death demanded.[24] But most symptomatic of the spirit of the time is the fact that the images and relics (both genuine and spurious) of the saints appeared prominently on the altar where they became the object of a special cult. The inversion is significant. Whereas in the early Church the relics were preserved below the altar, subject to it and blending with it into pure religious symbolism, in the Middle Ages they are above it, dominate it and form the focal point. They were incensed after the crucifix but before the altar itself. This exaggerated devotion to the saints, of which the extreme cult of their relics is a vivid manifestation, tended to replace, at least in the popular mind, Christ as unique Mediator between God and man. The tendency is especially significant in view of the fact that more and more Masses were composed and celebrated in honor of the saints.

The whole religious atmosphere of the late Middle Ages suggests uncontrolled and undisciplined development, a gradual but constant drift from the spirit of the early Church, a widening rift between theology and liturgy. The flamboyancy of Gothic art is reflected in worship. The Mass as a rite became *de facto* a 'spectacle' which the faithful were privileged to witness, rather than a religious act in which they had both a right and an obligation to share.

In the Eucharistic discourse of the sixth chapter of St. John's Gospel, Christ promised His disciples His Body and His Blood as a new food which would impart eternal life.[25] "Amen, Amen," He said, "unless you eat the flesh of the Son of Man, and drink His blood, you shall not have life in you." The new "bread of life" is faith and Eucharist—Word and Sacrament.

Those who would partake of this new heavenly manna with faith would live on forever and would rise one day to glory. The Last Supper fulfilled this solemn promise, for by offering His Body and Blood under the signs of bread and wine, Christ insured the abiding presence of this heavenly food in His Church. For the priesthood, which He then established, would constantly secure this new life-giving food, 'the memorial of the Lord.' Thus St. Paul at a later date sharply reminded the Christians of Corinth whose excesses he was admonishing, that the reception of the Eucharist proclaims "the death of the Lord, until He comes." And the Acts of the Apostles (2:42) describes those who were faithful to Christ as persevering "in the breaking of the bread." The stubborn adhesion of the Church to the Eucharist flows from the fact that through Christ it is her prime source of life and the pledge of the New Covenant into which God had called His people.

In the sources of the history of worship in the early Church the Eucharist appears central. On Sunday, the Day of Christ (hence, the Lord's Day), the Christians assembled in communal prayer, for the Church is a praying community, and essential to her prayer is the Eucharist. *The Apostolic Tradition* of St. Hippolytus describes how the bishop breaks the Bread in the assembly and distributes to each a fragment with the words,[26] "The Bread of Heaven in Christ Jesus," which is reverently accepted with the simple reply, "Amen"—"So be it." The atmosphere is marked by peace and fraternal charity, serenity and confidence. Later (Easter, 390–91) St. Ambrose in a didactic sermon to the Christian neophytes explains the Eucharist in these terms:[27]

Great indeed and venerable is the manna which rained down from heaven on the Jews. But hear further! Which is greater, the manna from heaven or the Body of Christ? Why of course the Body of the Christ who is the author of heaven. And, there is a further consideration. He who ate the manna died. He who shall eat this Body shall have his sins remitted and shall not die forever. Therefore, your "Amen" is not pointless, when you confess with your mind that you are receiving the Body of Christ. The priest says to you: "The Body of Christ!" And you say "Amen," that is, "You speak truly." What you confess with your tongue, hold with your mind.

From these two citations, which are generally representative of the Eucharistic thought and practice of the early Church, the essential picture of this Sacrament comes into clear focus— a new life-giving food under the symbols of bread and wine, imparted to the Christian assembly and accepted with the inner conviction of faith that this wondrous food is in truth the Body and Blood of Christ. St. Cyril of Jerusalem reminds the faithful that the Eucharistic service is at once communal banquet and solemn memorial, heralded by "a chanter, with a sacred melody inviting to the communion of the Holy Mysteries, and saying: 'O taste and see that the Lord is good.' "[28]

But throughout the Middle Ages under the stress of various cultural and theological influences which were to a great extent beyond the control of the Church, Eucharistic piety developed in a different direction. The following moments, which are very closely related to one another, can be distinguished. First, against the Semi-Arians the Church laid heavy stress on the dogma of the divinity of Christ, the Logos. Second, there is an exaggerated emphasis in the pastoral life of the Church on the

Eucharist as the sacrament of 'the Real Presence.' Third, as a consequence, the simple faithful gradually withdraw from the Eucharist, the dread sacrament, whose reception involved the very presence of "the Creator and Redeemer."[29] Thus the more the divine nature of Christ was underscored in the fierce anti-Arian polemic, the more His human nature faded from gaze. The more the divine nature was stressed, the more awesome and terrible became the Eucharist, the more overpowering the Real Presence. In the course of the centuries the sacrament of 'heavenly food' had become the sacrament of 'Real Presence.'

The development of the cult of the Real Presence is peculiarly medieval. There is scarcely a trace of it in Christian antiquity.[30] In proportion as the reception of Holy Communion diminished in frequency, the cult of the Eucharistic presence grew in intensity. Its most concrete expression—the elevation of the consecrated Bread and Wine—which emerged within the context of the liturgy itself, forms one of the most dramatic innovations in the Mass-rite of the medieval Church. The practice seems to have begun in the monastic observance of Cluny in the late eleventh century as a vivid reaction to the attack of Berengarius (d. 1088) on the Real Presence. The erroneous sacramental teaching of Peter Cantor (*ca.* 1199) was also an influential factor. But by the middle of the thirteenth century the elevation of Bread and Wine was universal throughout Europe. At the end of the Middle Ages 'seeing the Body of Christ'—gazing upon the elevated species at the solemn moment of its exaltation—had become almost a fetish. "It was the be-all and end-all of Mass devotion. See the Body of Christ at the consecration and be satisfied."[31]

The abuses which derived from this approach to Eucharistic

devotion were enormous, at times almost reaching the point of superstition. The belief was current among the people that on a day on which one had gazed upon the Sacred Host, one would not go hungry, be naked, lose one's eyesight, or die a sudden death; in the event, however, that "one should die suddenly without Communion, he would be considered as if he had received it."[32] At the approach of the consecration a bell in the steeple summoned the people from market, fields, shop, schoolroom and cloister to behold the elevated species. So intense was the desire to see the Sacred Host, that the priests strove mightily at the suggestion of the faithful to elevate it as high as possible,[33] to elevate it many times and for prolonged periods, to twist and turn it on high to the view of all.[34] It was indeed a dread moment of majesty and awe in which God stood revealed before man, and man communicated with God by sight. But as quickly as the people had assembled, they scattered.[35] The ecstasy was over and life was resumed.

In significant parallel to the development of the cult of the Eucharistic Presence is the institution of the feast of *Corpus Christi* through the instrumentality of Bl. Juliana of Liège (d. 1258) and Urban IV (d. 1264), who gave it universal approbation in his bull, *Transiturus* (August 11, 1264). The growth of Eucharistic piety was rapid. By the second half of the thirteenth century the monstrance had been devised; by the end of that century there is evidence of the *Corpus Christi* procession, and within the framework of this celebration Benediction of the Blessed Sacrament developed as a new religious rite. About a hundred years later, exposition of the Eucharist, though at first forbidden by episcopal synods, was already in vogue in Germany, while from the second half of the fourteenth century Eucharistic processions had become more and more common on the principal feast days, Easter, Pentecost and Christmas. Thus the cult of the Eucharist became a fixed part of Catholic piety.[36]

Devotion to the Eucharist is connatural to Catholicism. It flows from the dogma that Christ is truly present in the Sacrament of the Altar. That the medieval world despite certain peculiarities in her usage developed this cult is to her credit,[37] for it opened to Catholic piety new vistas which had been overlooked in the opening centuries of the Church. The sharp critiques which have been directed against medieval sacramentalism are mostly concerned with the abuse rather than the use of the Eucharist, with that uncontrolled tendency to separate the sacrificial and the sacramental, to concentrate too fixedly on the Eucharist as containing Christ rather than as conferring Him. The medieval preoccupation with Real Presence gradually led to a serious distortion in worship. More and more the faithful lost sight of the sacrificial character of the Mass, and more and more abstained from the reception of Holy Communion. In view of this grave desertion of the sacrament the Fourth Lateran Council (1215) in its twenty-first canon made yearly (Paschal) Communion obligatory on all adults. To adore the Sacred Host seemed more normal than to receive it as Sacrament, to gaze on it elevated at Mass more significant than to share in the Mass as a sacrifice. The right order of things had become inverted in that Real Presence took primacy over the sacramental and the sacrificial. That this devious line of development would lead to scandal and superstition was inevitable.

While the faithful neglected the sacrificial aspects of the Mass, they enhanced its impetrative value. All things were believed obtainable through the Mass.[38] Its fruits were most extensive, applicable to all the needs of life but very especially to the suffering souls of the faithful departed. The appeal was moving. Thus intention-Masses were increasingly demanded; and, in consequence, priests and altars were multiplied. The ancient idea that there should be but one altar and one sacrifice in one community vanished. Private masses with private intentions came more and more into vogue. Their celebration by the so-called 'Mass-priests' was generally confined to private chapels away from the community and appeared out of harmony with the simplicity of the ancient Church. The fact that to each of these 'devotional' Masses a pecuniary offering was attached as support for the 'Mass-priest,' offered rich soil for the growth of scandal. The intrusion of the private and the subjective is further illustrated by the wide variety of votive Masses which were introduced more and more at this time to be celebrated in honor of the saints or on behalf of special intentions. Thus the *Missa de tempore,* the Mass of the day, the common liturgical text of the universal Church, yielded more and more to the votive Mass as an expression of 'private' devotion. At the same time the liturgical calendar became overgrown with feasts of the saints which tended to displace the commemoration of the great mysteries of salvation history.

There has come down to us from the Middle Ages a series of liturgical treatises which offer valuable insight into the medieval conception of the structure and meaning of the liturgy. These works, dominated by the Alexandrian spirit (allegory) of biblical exegesis, are for the most part devoted to discovering the ultimate spiritual reality hidden beneath the external rubrics of the Mass and the sacraments. Candles, incense, wine, water, vestments, oil, fire, and the other ceremonial appurtenances were made to yield in their spiritual, allegorical, sense a mystical meaning which was valued as transcending by far the commonplace realities of this world.

These 'allegorical insights' only served to obscure in the minds of the laity the true theology of the Mass. Inspired neither by historical research nor biblical theology, they were arbitrary, capricious, mostly improvised, grossly imaginative, "wedded to the extension of the rememorative type of allegory." The Mass, more and more "looked upon as a holy drama, a play performed before the eyes of the participants ... a dramatic presentation," was conceived by these medieval commentators as a patchwork of allegorical vignettes spun out of historical episodes and biblical personages.[39] The development which we find in these allegorizing commentaries is far from inculcating liturgical piety or situating worship within the context of salvation history or Christian antiquity.

I cite here one example to illustrate this literary genre. It is taken from Innocent III's (d. 1216) *De sacro altaris mysterio,* a treatise on the mystery of the Mass, in which the pope is explaining the allegorical significance of the bishop's greeting (kiss) of the altar:[40]

Then the bishop approaches and kisses the altar. This signifies that Christ, when He came, joined the holy Church to Himself according to the wedding song: "Let him kiss me with the kiss of his mouth."

Mouth is joined to mouth in the act of kissing. And in Christ not only is the humanity united to the divinity, but also bride is joined to groom, acccording to the prophetic saying: "He has adorned me with a diadem like a bridegroom, he has bedecked me with jewels like a bride."

The imaginative explanation which Innocent gives here of the simple rubric is artificial and exaggerated, certainly far from what subsequent historical research has shown about the ultimate origins of this ancient greeting of the altar; but it is perfectly in accord with the medieval predilection for the allegorical and the mystical.

The various aberrations, distortions and deviations in the liturgy of the Mass which arose in the course of the Middle Ages reached a critical stage in the fifteenth century, the century in which the clamor for reform had reached a crescendo. The liturgical problems of the late medieval world were not so much theological as pastoral. For the Catholic theology of the Mass, if not fully worked out in all its implications, was certainly correct and in line with dogma. The question here was practical rather than theoretical. There was need of introducing the theology of the Mass into pastoral life, of educating the clergy and the laity in liturgical piety, of removing abuse and every suspicion of abuse which had crept into the order of Catholic worship over the centuries. The badly needed liturgical reform should have started with the clergy, but in view of the meager priestly education, it was hardly capable of instituting a liturgical renaissance. Ecclesiastical reform requires intelligent, courageous leadership, and there was very little of this at that time. It must also be supported by ecclesiastical administrators who know how to bring their authority to bear on the most pressing problems of the day. Such men were unfortunately lacking.

In the fifteenth century two ecumenical councils, Constance (1414–18) and Basle (1431–39), were convoked with the avowed purpose of reforming the Church 'in head and members.' On the very eve of the Reformation a third ecumenical council, Lateran V (1512–17), closed after having sat in session for more than five years. The acts of these councils which have come down to us testify to the quantity of the words which were spoken by the Fathers in these crowded, ecumenical assemblies. Everyone seems to have had his say. Yet that these 'reform' councils decreed virtually nothing of importance for the restoration and the renewal of the liturgy is unfortunate. It is unforgivable that their decrees on ecclesiastical reformation were either ignored or discarded.

The twenty-first session (June 9, 1435) of the Council of Basle, a part of the conciliar proceedings never accepted by the Holy See, did promulgate certain liturgical reforms which are indicative of the trends of these times. A close inspection of these conciliar prescriptions shows the pathetic state to which liturgical observance had come in this century. For example, it lists these abuses as common to various churches:[41]

. . . the *Credo in unum Deum,* the symbol and profession of our faith, is not completely sung to the end; the Preface or the Lord's Prayer is omitted; and in the churches worldly music accompanies the singing; even private Mass is celebrated without a server and its secret part is said in such a subdued voice that it cannot be heard by the by-standers. . . .

The synod also condemned the irreverent disturbance which the Chapters cause in the churches. "This holy synod forbids Chapters from meeting during the time of the principal Mass, especially on solemn feast days, from transacting capitular or other business, unless perhaps the need be clearly urgent."[42]

The final decree of the session is rich in insight into the worldly character of certain ecclesiastical practices which the fifteenth century had inherited from an earlier day. The Council rejects:

that abuse so recurrent in different churches. Here, on the occasion of certain annual festivities, some with mitre, crosier and episcopal vestments impart a blessing as bishops do. Others are dressed like kings and dukes. In some regions this is called the feast of fools, of the innocents, of young boys. Some engage in the mask and comedy. Some form groups of men and women into choral bands of dancers. The effect is a comic spectacle. Some, right there in the church, spread banquets and feasts.[43]

When these abuses (and others) are considered in light of the grotesque art, ornamentation and music which were making their way into the churches at this time, the effect is alarming.

Throughout the century before the Reformation liturgical reform invariably centered about the external, the rubrical and the procedural. Since elimination of abuse was central, the reform was generally negative. There is no mention of the interiority of the liturgy and its efficaciousness in fostering sanctity and piety which, as fundamental to any renewal of laity and clergy alike, were the most pressing needs of that desperate hour.

On the eve of the Reformation Catholic worship was in grave crisis. Quantitatively it was vigorous, and to be found on all sides in splendor and magnificence; but qualitatively it was debilitated, for corporate worship in the full sense of that term had almost vanished from the Church. Louis Bouyer[44] reports a very significant conversation between two of the most influential English churchmen of that day, Cranmer and Gardiner, when both were still orthodox Catholic priests.

Cranmer said, "How sad it is that the people in the nave of the church do not understand anything about what is being celebrated in the sanctuary!" And Gardiner answered, "Don't worry about that, it has never occurred to them that they might want to understand it!"

And Père Bouyer rightly adds, "How distressing it is for us now to consider that it was the future heretic who had the more truly Catholic reaction!" This conversation, an epitome of the liturgical crisis just before the Reformation, clearly marks out the wall of separation between sanctuary and nave, between priest and people, which the reformers were resolved to smash to pieces.

If it be true that the Reformation, as Martin Luther (d. 1546) conceived it, was a Bible revolution, it is equally true (and necessarily so) that it was a liturgical revolution. For Luther, Bible and liturgy, like all aspects of Christian life and faith, were intimately connected. "The holy sacraments," he wrote,[45] "and articles of faith rightly demand that they be founded and preserved only through the divine scriptures. . . . The question is not about what has been done, but about how it is supposed to be done. The saints could err in their writings and sin in their lives, but the Scriptures cannot err." It was, therefore, Luther's intent to construct his concept of Christianity on the Bible, concretely on the principle that salvation is through faith alone and not through human works, that faith rests on the Word of God and not on the word of man. It was obvious that this way of looking at things would be operative in his reform of the liturgy.

Since faith in the Word of God alone is efficacious in the order of salvation, the liturgy is only relevant to the Christian inasmuch as it is evangelical, serving both Word and faith. In itself it has no efficacy, at least in the traditional sense of being an *opus operatum*.[46] But it can and should stimulate faith, a service which it renders only to the extent that it expresses outwardly the Word. In view of this concept of the liturgical order Luther eliminated all the sacraments save baptism and the eucharist, keeping these because both were intimately connected with profession of faith and both were clearly based on Scripture. In their own way both preached an eloquent sermon on the Word of God, faith in Christ and Christian commitment.

When applied to the Mass, Luther's theology of the Word had a transforming effect on its essential character. For by stressing the inefficacy of good works and the uniqueness of the sacrifice of Christ, the sacrificial aspect of the Mass was virtually extinguished. In the new evangelical liturgy the Mass was a religious rite with a double aspect: *testament,* because of the promise of Christ, and *sacrament,* because of His Body and Blood. But the testament—Christ's solemn promise of forgiveness of sin—exceeds the sacrament, to which it gives both life and meaning. Considered from this double aspect the Mass appeared as a benefit received from God rather than as a gift which men bestowed on Him.[47] In no sense could it be called a propitiatory sacrifice, "the idolatry of the pseudo-church."[48] This emphatic rejection of the sacrificial character of Catholic worship is illustrated by his emphatic (and scornful) rejection of the Canon of the Mass in which the elements both of propitiation and sacrifice are prominent and explicit.[49] As a liturgical act, the Mass had become for Luther a function of faith.[50]

Accordingly, the Mass should find its center in the faith. It should be a Gospel-proclamation "which is nothing but a proclamation of God's grace and of the forgiveness of all sins";[51] and since the heart of the Gospel is in the solemn testament of Christ to all mankind, there, too, should be the heart of the Mass. Thus Luther wrote of the Mass:[52]

[It] was instituted to preach and praise Christ, to glorify his sufferings and all his grace and goodness, so that we may be moved to love him, to hope and believe in him, and thus, in addition to this word or sermon, to receive an outward sign, that is the sacrament.

The liturgy, therefore, should terminate in stronger witness to Christ by deeper personal gratitude, hope and faith in Him whose saving testament was proclaimed at the very moment that the words of institution (consecration) were uttered. This is what Luther meant when he said: "the principal purpose of any service of worship is the teaching and preaching of the Word of God."[53]

The new liturgy was envisioned in terms of evangelical simplicity and its ability to communicate the mind and the spirit of Christ to the faithful. It was made adaptable and flexible to meet diversity of time and place. Consequently it could not be bound by the traditional legal forms and formalities which were characteristic of the Church. Because the liturgy in its inner being is kerygmatic, it must be didactic; and because it is didactic, it should be intelligible.[54] To celebrate 'private Mass'—apart from the presence of a congregation to hear the Word proclaimed—seemed to Luther an intolerable abomination.[55] Committed to the Gospel which it proclaims, the liturgy of the Word dominated the liturgy of the Sacrament. In broad outline this was the ideal which Luther proposed to his evangelical congregations. Its realization was rarely perfect.

If the medieval Church had neglected the Word, Luther had not; but in his new liturgical order the Sacrament, which the Church of his day treasured, was relegated to a secondary place. His reform terminated in the abolition of the traditional priesthood, propitiatory sacrifice and the sacramental system as it had been known up to then. It is the theologian's task to assay and appraise the doctrinal significance of this revolutionary aspect of Luther's work. But the point of interest here is that his reformed order of divine worship was the product of a liturgical renovation in the direction of the evangelical, the popular and the intelligible. In the liturgy of the late Middle Ages he did not discover a mode of public prayer consonant with the Gospel. Weighed down by the accumulation of the centuries, the old method seemed effete, capable only with difficulty of achieving the fullness of its purpose. That the Church should have realistically reformed her liturgy in the fifteenth century (and even earlier) goes without saying. But it did not do this! A revolution, therefore, came which in its enthusiasm for an ideal tried to eliminate the ancient priesthood and sacrifice of the Church.

In the late summer and autumn of 1521 Wittenberg was in liturgical ferment. On September 22nd Melanchthon celebrated an evangelical Lord's Supper; a month later Mass ceased to be celebrated in the Augustinian convent of which Luther had been a member. On Christmas Day in the Castle Church, Andreas Carlstadt (d. 1541), without vestments, led 2,000 people in divine worship reformed along such radical lines that it was clearly no longer the sacrifice of the Mass but a simple Gospel service in which communion was distributed under both species. In 1522 Luther's New Testament appeared in the vernacular and quickly went through many editions. Within a few years his *German Mass* (1526) was being widely disseminated in those parts of Central Europe which were sympathetic to the new evangelism. Similar phenomena were taking place in France and England where the core of the movement was invariably twofold: vernacular Bible and vernacular liturgy.

In the twenty-five years from 1521 to 1545 (the year in

which the Council of Trent opened) the Church had witnessed the beginning of this revolution and its progressive development. By the middle of the sixteenth century it must have been clear to any shrewd, realistic observer that this evangelical movement would not wane and die of its own inner ineptitude, and that it could neither be suppressed nor overthrown by force. In reading the ecclesiastical history of this period it is surprising to note that no progressive program was presented by the Church as an effective, enlightened balance to these new ideas. At times there seems to have been a sense of expectancy that things somehow or other, perhaps even spontaneously, would change for the better; or that the armed force of emperor Charles V would ultimately prove decisive. It did not however! The Church was forced to face the issues, even to the point of waiting four hundred years to solve them.

In an earlier chapter we have seen how the problem of the vernacular Bible was left unsolved by the Council of Trent. Its refusal to meet this issue meant that the liturgy of the Word would continue along the unreal lines formulated in Late Antiquity. The liturgy of the Sacrament, however, fared better, perhaps because the Reformers had set forth their new ideas on the traditional sacramental and sacrificial systems in such wise that the Fathers could not overlook the theological issues which they raised. It was their obligation to propose sound Catholic doctrine and to defend it. That the Council approached this aspect of its work seriously and efficiently is a matter of history. Its decrees on the sacraments and the Mass did much to eliminate the many erroneous ideas and abuses which had grown up about these chief channels of sanctification. The

Council gave the Church a reasonably clear statement of what
its faith should be; it did not answer all dogmatic questions;
and the answers which it gave were not always perfectly formulated. But the sum of its teaching was to prove of considerable
advantage in the subsequent education of the faithful. The
most valid critique of Tridentine theology must be directed
against the rigidity of the subsequent theologians of the Council whose historical perspective was so restricted.

The vast question of liturgical reform—and by all standards
it was indeed vast—was handled in a minimal way. Like the
Bible, the Roman Missal and the other liturgical books remained in Latin. The mind of the Council on this point is
clearly embodied in the seventh chapter of the twenty-second
session (September 17, 1562):[56] "Though the Mass contains
much instruction for the faithful, it has, nevertheless, not been
deemed advisable by the Fathers that it should be celebrated
everywhere in the vernacular tongue." Thus, the Mass, considered to play an educational role in spiritual life, was forced
to use an unintelligible medium of communication. And this
restriction of the use of the vernacular was directed against the
Reformers whose worship was in the mother tongue. It was indeed a clever counter-thrust, but an expensive one—four centuries of a Latin liturgy!

Certain obvious abuses were stamped out by conciliar decree;[57] for example, avarice in connection with Mass-stipends.
Worldly music was eliminated from Church-services, the quality of priests allowed to celebrate in public closely controlled,
and the dignified observance of liturgical solemnities regulated.
Of importance was the Council's statement that "at each Mass

the faithful who are present should communicate, not only in spiritual desire but also by the sacramental partaking of the Eucharist."[58] Apart from certain striking exceptions, for example the Eucharistic activity of the German Jesuits and their sodalities, this valuable prescription remained a dead letter until the days of Pope St. Pius X. Further, the Council urged pastors "either themselves or through others, to explain frequently during the celebration of the Mass some of the things read during the Mass, and that among other things they explain some mystery of this most holy sacrifice."[59] Lastly, in the twenty-fifth session the Council provided for the revision of the Roman Missal and Breviary at the hands of the pope.

The execution of this latter decree was not to be the work of Pius IV, who died December 9, 1565, slightly more than two years after the Council had closed. The arduous task, therefore, passed to his successor, the Dominican pope St. Pius V, who presented the Church on July 14, 1570 with "the new Roman Missal restored by decree of the Sacred Council of Trent and published by order of Pope Pius V." This Missal was intended to be the one, uniform book of worship for the entire Latin Church. Basically it was "the Missal according to the usage of the Roman Curia" defined and limited by the practice of the papal master of ceremonies, John Burchard of Strassburg. Its spirit and structure were determined by two factors: the *Roman,* not only in its liturgical text and rite, but also in the liturgical calendar around which they were constructed; and the *traditional,* that is, the practice of the ancient Church of Rome as a guiding norm. Thus in turning to the distant past to find its model and inspiration, it neglected both intervening development and contemporary need. It did not regard organic growth as a liturgical factor worthy of consideration. This Missal with certain modifications has remained with the Church to this day.[60]

By the opening years of the sixteenth century the Roman Breviary had become a complicated jungle overgrown with useless repetitions, unreasonable extensions, hagiographical legend and various external matters that made its recitation an intolerable burden to the clergy. As early as the pontificate of Clement VII (1532–34), the Franciscan Cardinal Francisco de Quiñones (d. 1540) had been requested to prepare a revised breviary, a work which he accomplished between 1529 and 1535. The result was a simplified, corrected, reformed breviary, an innovation which, while breaking in certain respects with tradition, was sufficiently conservative in many of its features and at the same time answered a pressing need. It appeared in 1535 with the approval of Paul III whose brief described it as "a Roman Breviary put together and edited especially from Sacred Scripture and reliable lives of the saints." The emphasis, therefore, was on the Bible and Church History. The lessons from the Scripture were divided "with a real knowledge of the contents of the Sacred Books and with concern for giving nourishment to the spirit . . . All the purely accidental and fortuitous older divisions" were discarded.[61] In his revision of the *Sanctorale*—the hagiographical portion of the Office—care was taken to remove the legendary, the spectacular and the naïve. Dignity, prudence and reserve were his chief aims. For twenty-two years the breviary of Quiñones was in vogue. Far from perfect, it was realistically conceived as a progressive advance in liturgical reform. It was appreciated, especially by those priests who had a busy apostolic life. Within a year it had gone through eleven printings in different parts of Europe.

On August 8, 1558 Pope Paul IV in secret consistory set it aside, probably on the basis of personal considerations.[62] A new breviary was to be prepared which would represent the ancient manner and, therefore, the traditional mode of reciting the canonical hours. Once again the practice of the Roman *Curia* was to prove decisive in the reformation of liturgical books, for the new breviary was to be the revised and restored Roman breviary—"the traditional breviary of the Roman Curia as it had been printed since 1474." At the Council of Trent the ideas of Paul IV were sponsored by the Spaniards whose mind prevailed; and "the mind of the Spanish prelates was also that of the Roman Curia."[63]

The chief opponent of the new breviary of Quiñones was Juan de Arze, Spanish theologian and canon of Palencia, who presented the Fathers of Trent in 1551 with his "Memorial on the Removal of the New Breviary." Here, in eighteen chapters, a sharp criticism was delivered with gusto against both the spirit and the method of Quiñones' work. His critique of the prominent position which the cardinal had assigned to the reading of Holy Scripture is highly instructive to those who are currently interested in the reform of the breviary. It shows the canon's mind to be perfectly in tune with the medieval world rather than with 'the novelties' of his own day. For him the new breviary is more concerned with reading the Bible than it is with praying for and with the Church. And this practice he finds to be out of harmony with the venerable tradition of the Church

which has entrusted the study of Holy Scripture to her principal ministers, while to the more simple clergy (*rudiores clerici*)
she has given the task of psalmody. Their work is very different from that "of the doctors, the exegetes and the masters." For
the uneducated cleric (*idiota clericus*) "who at times knows
nothing more than Latin grammar," for the mass of the clergy
(*vulgus clericorum*), the indiscriminate reading of the Bible
can only be harmful. Especially worthless to them is much
reading of St. Paul. Therefore, for these and other considerations the new breviary must be set aside.[64] In these days when
Bible reading has become a normal part of Catholic life, one
cannot help but wonder at the mentality of our forefathers for
whom this practice could be such a potential source of evil.

The opinion of Canon de Arze prevailed not only with the
Fathers of Trent who handed the reform of the breviary over
to the papacy, but also with Pius IV and St. Pius V. The reformed breviary, the "*Breviarium Romanum* restored by a decree of the sacred council of Trent and published by order of
Pius V," was finished in record time (1566). It first appeared
in 1568, and its use throughout the universal Church was implemented by a brief of St. Pius V, *Quod a nobis*, dated July 1,
1568. This breviary is currently the subject of a thorough reform whose spirit is in so many respects akin to that which
once animated the efforts of Cardinal Quiñones. Apropos of
this revision the observation of the Second Vatican Council is
worthy of note: "Readings from sacred scripture shall be arranged [in the breviary] so that the riches of God's word may
be easily accessible in more abundant measure." If not ironic,
this decree is certainly indicative of the reversals that come with
time, and that give ample pause for reflection.

On January 22, 1588 Pope Sixtus V set up the Sacred Congregation of Rites as a tribunal for the future defense, protection and interpretation of the rubrics. Its function was not to create new forms but rather to preserve the old ones. In fact, the erection of this special tribunal inaugurated an epoch in the history of the liturgy which has rightly been characterized as the "Period of codified Liturgy and rubrical Rule," a period when the science of rubrics and liturgical casuistry came into prominence. Throughout the three and one-half centuries since its inauguration this stabilizing factor in the Roman rite has stultified, frozen and ossified the forms of liturgical worship. But in thus holding the Catholic liturgy within definite limits it preserved it from the decadence of both Baroque and Romantic influences.

In terms of the developments which have been taking place in Catholic life since the close of the Council of Trent over four hundred years ago, the Vatican *Constitution on the Liturgy* becomes highly significant both as a reform decree and as a progressive document. It forms a turning point in the inner life of the Church and her worship. Finally, in our day, the task to which the ecumenical councils of the fifteenth and sixteenth centuries would not set their hand, has been performed. This Constitution is a true *reformatio* in the best sense of the word. By intent and purpose it envisions a restoration of the liturgy to its pristine form as a vital element in Catholic life.

The *Constitution* stresses four points which are pivots of Catholic worship. First, the Church is described as the Mystical Body of Christ. "Every liturgical celebration . . . is an action of Christ the priest and of his body which is the Church" (7). Second, the function of Christ in the public prayer of the

Church is sacerdotal. "The liturgy is considered as an exercise of the priestly office of Christ" (7). Third, the Word of God is part of divine worship. "The two parts which . . . go to make up the Mass, namely the liturgy of the Word and the liturgy of the Eucharist are so closely connected with each other that they form but one single act of worship" (56). And, fourth, priest and people pray as a unity. "Liturgical services are not private functions, but are the celebrations of the Church, which is the 'sacrament of unity,' namely the holy people united and ordered under their bishop" (26).

The late medieval problem of worship has certainly been solved in our day, at least on paper. But it must not remain a paper solution. The history of the Church has known too many such theoretical approaches to her problems. The Council has declared the liturgy to be "the summit towards which the activity of the Church is directed" (10). A sentiment such as this has rarely been expressed in the ecumenical councils of the past. It is our duty and privilege to give it the reality of form and substance in the life of the Church which so badly needs the vitality of this new apostolate of worship.

NOTES

[1] Luther, too, recognized Word and Sacrament, but with a different emphasis. Thus he writes: "The Word, the Word (I say) merits more regard than the whole sacrament with all that it is and can do, for the Word is the chief thing. . . ." Cf. M. Luther, *Commentary on the Alleged Imperial Edict* (1531), ed. L. W. Spitz, *Luther's Works* 34, *Career of the Reformer* 4 (Philadelphia 1960), p. 82.

[2] Cf. on the liturgical development of the anicent Church, J. Jungmann, S.J., *The Early Liturgy* (Notre Dame 1959), pp. 31–8.

[3] *Ignatius to the Philadelphians* 4, tr. A. A. Kleist, S.J., *Ancient Christian Writers* 1 (Westminster 1946), p. 86.

[4] Cf. on the character of these 'distractions' R. E. McNally, S.J., *The Reform of the Church, op. cit.,* pp. 73 ff.

[5] "Die Abwehr des germanischen Arianismus und der Umbruch der religiösen Kultur im frühen Mittelalter," *Zeitschrift für katholische Theologie* 69 (1947) 36–99, poorly translated in *Pastoral Liturgy* (New York 1962), pp. 1–63.

[6] *Ibid.,* p. 1.

[7] Cf. A. Mayer, "Die Liturgie und der Geist der Gothik," *Jahrbuch für Liturgiewissenschaft* 6 (1926), p. 97: "The path, which the Catholic liturgy —inasmuch as it remains a living reality with the people—follows to this day, is in the direction which the Gothic defined. True to that spirit, it set the individual free from the community and released the subject from the objective form."

[8] Cf. J. Jungmann, S.J., "Liturgical Life on the Eve of the Reformation," *Pastoral Liturgy,* pp. 64–80.

[9] Cf. C. J. Barry, O.S.B., ed., *Readings in Church History* Vol. 1, p. 48.

[10] We have the amusing example of a Bavarian priest reported to Pope Zachary (741–52) for having used in his very poor knowledge of Latin the following baptismal formula: "Baptizo te in nomine *Patria* et *Filia* et Spiritus sancti." Cf. *Enchiridion Symbolorum,* ed., A. Schönmetzer, S.J., ed. (Freiburg 1963) 588, p. 198.

[11] Cf. C. Mohrmann, *Liturgical Latin* (Washington 1957), pp. 1–29.

[12] R. E. McNally, S.J., "The 'Tres Linguae Sacrae' in Early Irish Bible Exegesis," *Theological Studies* 19 (1958), pp. 395–403.

[13] *Ibid.,* p. 395: This tradition reached "as far back as Hilary of Poitiers (*ca.* 315–67), who very especially commended Hebrew, Greek, and Latin, the languages through which the mystery of God's will, the announcement of His kingdom, and the suprascription of the cross were transmitted to the world." (Cf. *Tractatus super psalmos: Instructio psalmorum* 15). The same tradition is continued and developed by Augustine (*In Iohannis evangelium tract,* 117, 4) ". . . Hebrew is a symbol of the Law of the Jews, Greek of the Wisdom of the Gentiles, and Latin of the Empire of the Romans."

[14] C. A. Lewis, *The Silent Recitation of the Canon of the Mass* (Bay St. Louis 1962), pp. 35 ff.

[15] Amalarius of Metz (d. *ca.* 850), one of the most influential of the Caro-

lingian commentators on the liturgy, refers to the Canon as "the special prayer of the priests." "Wherefore," he writes, "seeing that this prayer pertains
especially to the priest, the priest alone enters into it. Let him recite it in
secret." Cf. *Eclogae de Ordine Romano* 24, ed., J. M. Hanssens, S.J., *Amalari
Episcopi Opera Omnia Liturgica* 3 (Vatican 1950), pp. 255–56.

[16] For example, "in 1698, Mathurin Savary, bishop of Séez, in a pastoral
letter to his clergy, threatened suspension to any priest who should say the
canon otherwise than in a low voice." Cf. A. A. King, *Liturgy of the Roman
Church* (Milwaukee 1957), p. 432.

[17] For example, the Catholic reformer Johannes Busch, O.P. (d. 1480) re-
counts that he burnt a German translation of the Canon which he found in
a convent of nuns. "I do not approve," he wrote, "of the simple laity, whether
men or women, having such ancient and sacred books in German." Cf. A.
Franz, *Die Messe im deutschen Mittelalter* (Freiburg 1902), p. 632, n. 3.

[18] As late as 1851 the Bishop of Langre in France was denied permission by
the Sacred Congregation of Rites (June 6, 1851) to have the Ordinary of the
Mass translated into French. Permission to translate the entire Mass text was
first given by St. Pius X, in 1912. Cf. C. A. Lewis, *op. cit.,* pp. 66–7.

[19] Cf. *ibid.,* p. 65. Pius VI (1775–99) showed similar irritation with the
declarations of the Synod of Pistoia (1794) in favor of the vernacular. Cf.
Enchiridion Symbolorum 1733. Cf. L. Bouyer, *Liturgical Piety* (Notre Dame
1954), pp. 51 ff.

[20] Cf. J. Jungmann, S.J., "Liturgical Life in the Baroque Period," *Pastoral
Liturgy,* p. 87, who characterizes the liturgy at this time in these words: "The
liturgy is part of the legal ordinance which has to be observed, not something
which people really live."

[21] The whole question of the *Missa versus populum* in the primitive Church
has been posed once again. Cf. L. Bouyer, *Rite and Man* (Notre Dame 1963),
pp. 151–88, and T. F. Matthews, "P. Bouyer on Sacred Space: A Re-appraisal,"
The Downside Review 82 (1964), pp. 277–80.

[22] Cf. F. J. Dölger, "Die Heiligkeit des Altars und ihre Begründung im
christlichen Altertum," *Antike und Christentum* 2 (1930), p. 183.

[23] Cf. J. Jungmann, S.J., *The Mass of the Roman Rite,* Vol. 1 (New York
1950), p. 256.

[24] Cf. R. E. McNally, S.J., "Beata Passio," *Worship* 38 (1964), pp. 120–25.

[25] Cf. R. Brown, S.S., "The Eucharist and Baptism in St. John," *Proceedings
of the Eighth Annual Convention of the Society of Catholic Teachers of
Sacred Doctrine* (Philadelphia 1962), pp. 14–33.

[26] Cf. C. J. Barry, *op. cit.,* p. 52.

²⁷ *De Sacramentis* 4, 5, 24.

²⁸ *Mystagogical Catechesis* 4, 20, F. L. Cross, ed., *St. Cyril of Jerusalem's Christian Sacraments* (London 1951), pp. 78–9.

²⁹ This language is typical. Thus "the provincial council of Oxford in 1222 decreed: 'Let the laity be frequently reminded that whenever they see the Body of the Lord . . . they immediately kneel down to their Creator and Redeemer. . . . And let them do this especially at the elevation of the Host. . . .'" T. E. Bridgett, *A History of the Holy Eucharist in Great Britain* (London 1908), p. 99.

³⁰ Normal in the ancient Church is the Eucharist as sacrifice and sacrament. The Eucharist, however, was reserved for Communion of the sick and Viaticum.

³¹ Cf. J. Jungmann, S.J., *The Mass of the Roman Rite*, Vol. 1, p. 121.

³² A. Franz, *op. cit.*, p. 103, n. 3. These peculiar ideas were falsely attributed to no one less than St. Augustine!

³³ "It could happen—as it did in England—that if the celebrant did not elevate the host high enough, the people would cry out: 'Hold up, Sir John, hold up. Heave it a little higher.'" Cf. J. Jungmann, S.J., *The Mass of the Roman Rite*, Vol. 1, p. 121, n. 101.

³⁴ "I do not see why this is done," Matthew of Cracow remarked in one of his cynical moments, "unless it be to cheat the simple people out of their money." Cf. A. Franz, *op. cit.*, p. 105, n. 1.

³⁵ Thus the Franciscan Michael of Hungary declared that the people rush out of the church "as if they had seen the devil." Note, too, the pointed remarks of Heinrich of Langenstein cited by H. Thurston, S.J., "Benediction of the Blessed Sacrament," *The Month* 97 (1901), pp. 592–93.

³⁶ Cf. A. G. Martimort, *L'Eglise en prière* (Tournai 1961), pp. 462–70.

³⁷ Among these peculiarities might be cited practices such as using the Host in the ordeal by fire, burying the Host with the faithful, sealing the Host in the altar stone, etc.

³⁸ A. Franz, *op. cit.*, pp. 36–72.

³⁹ Cf. J. Jungmann, S.J., *The Mass of the Roman Rite* 1, 107, 111.

⁴⁰ PL 217, 807B. In general, the pope's treatise is "a healthy reaction to the increased overloading of the interpretation of the Mass with so many diverse elements." Cf. J. Jungmann, S.J., *The Mass of the Roman Rite* Vol. 1, p. 111.

⁴¹ J. Alberigo, et al., ed., *Conciliorum Oecumenicorum Decreta* (Basel 1962), p. 467.

⁴² *Ibid.*, p. 468.

⁴³ *Ibid.*

[44] L. Bouyer, *Liturgical Piety*, p. 2.

[45] *The Misuse of the Mass* 3 (1521), trans. by F. C. Ahrens, *Luther's Works* 36, *Word and Sacrament* 2 (Philadelphia 1959), pp. 135–36.

[46] For if the Sacrament "is merely an *opus operatum*," wrote Luther, "it works only harm everywhere; it must become an *opus operantis* . . . It is not enough that the sacrament be merely completed (that is, *opus operatum*); it must also be used in faith (that is, *opus operantis*)." Cf. *The Blessed Sacrament of the Holy and True Body of Christ* 20 (1519), trans. by J. J. Schindel (rev., E. T. Bachmann), *Luther's Works* 35, *Word and Sacrament* 1 (Philadelphia 1960), p. 63.

[47] *Treatise on the New Testament* 19–20 (1520), trans. by J. J. Schindel (rev., E. T. Bachmann), *Luther's Works* 35, *Word and Sacrament* 1, pp. 93–94: "For a testament is not *beneficium acceptum, sed datum;* it does not take benefit from us, but brings benefit to us . . . Here there is no *officium* but *beneficium,* no work or service but reception and benefit alone."

[48] Cf. V. Vajta, *Luther on Worship* (Philadelphia 1958), pp. 62–63.

[49] *Ibid.,* p. 62. Luther wrote: "Yield to the gospel, O Canon, and give room to the Holy Spirit, since thou art merely a human word."

[50] Cf. *Treatise on the New Testament* 34, *ed. cit.,* p. 108: "For the mass is best to him who believes most, and it serves only to increase faith."

[51] *Ibid.,* 32, p. 106.

[52] *Ibid.,* p. 105.

[53] J. Pelikan, "Luther and the Liturgy," *More about Luther* (Decorah 1958), p. 29.

[54] At first, Luther was not opposed to a Latin liturgy. "I have not the slightest wish," he wrote, "to abolish the use of Latin in public worship." Circumstances, however, forced him to take a more realistic view of a vernacular liturgy.

[55] More than once Luther made his mind clear on this point. On August 1, 1521 he wrote to Melanchthon: "I will never say another private Mass"; and to Spalatin on October 1, 1521: "It is a crime for the mass to be celebrated privately, since it is called *Synaxis* (assembly) and communion. The order of Christ and Paul commands that it should be celebrated often in public and with a congregation gathered for the proclamation of the Word, that is in rememberance of Christ." Cf. *Luther's Works* 48, *Letters* 1, tr. G. C. Krodel (Philadelphia 1963), pp. 281, 317.

[56] Cf. H. J. Schroeder, *Canons and Decrees of the Council of Trent* (London 1941), p. 148.

57 Cf. *ibid.,* pp. 150–52: "Decree concerning the things to be observed and avoided in the celebration of Mass."

58 Cf. *ibid.,* p. 147: Session 22, Chapter 6.

59 Cf. *ibid.,* p. 148.

60 J. Jungmann, S.J., *The Mass of the Roman Rite,* Vol. 1, pp. 133 ff.

61 Cf. P. Salmon, O.S.B., *The Breviary through the Centuries* (Collegeville 1962), p. 84.

62 Nothing that broke with tradition ever pleased this dyspeptic old tyrant.

63 P. Batiffol, *History of the Roman Breviary* (New York 1898) pp. 255, 264.

64 I am much indebted here to J. Jungmann, S.J., "Warum ist das Reformbrevier des Kardinals Quinonez Gescheitert?", *Zeitschrift für kath. Theologie* 78 (1956), pp. 101–102.

5 * Christi

THE CORNER-STONE OF THE CHRISTIAN LIFE of the spirit is Christ, "the Alpha and the Omega, the beginning and the end" of all supernatural existence. As Saviour of men, He is their Lord; and, as Lord, He presides over the destinies of those who belong to Him. Apart from Christ there is no holiness in this world; but men, united to Him, are thereby united to God in friendship. And in this wondrous union of God and man, the heart of Christian sanctity is to be found. But the saving action of Christ extends further, into the realms of life and wisdom which are also involved in holiness. For, as Head of the Mystical Body, He is the origin of the new life which His members live; and, as Prophet, he is the source of the precious truth by which they are saved. Basic to the Christian religion are these three primordial realities—ontological union with God by grace, supernatural life through Christ, and true wisdom from the Word. They are the ultimate foundation of the spiritual life and represent the gifts of God to man, the capital and unique achievement of Christ in this world.

But fundamental to 'the reasonable service' which the Christian faith requires is the right understanding of the author of these gifts, Christ, true God and true man, Priest and Mediator of the New Law. He is the bridge, the arch which spans and joins the human and the divine; He is the rising, ascending Lord who is drawing humanity with Him upward to God, the common Father of all men. This Christ, the image according to which man was created, is also the image according to which he is to be restored. This restoration is the special work of Christ.

It is the pastoral office of the Church to communicate this Christ to men not only in the mystical order of grace but also in the sapiential order of truth. Each generation of Christians must be introduced to that Christ whom the preceding generation has learned to know from the faithful witness of those who went before it. The chief concern of the Church in her pastoral life is the acceptance of Christ by men; but without knowledge there can be no acceptance; and since Christian knowledge is faith, it must be built on the sacred text in which the Saviour stands publicly revealed.[1] In God's open manifestation of His Son to mankind the true picture of Christ is discovered. Here is the middle point on which the teaching office of the Church concentrates; here is the absolute center from which the spiritual life takes its first beginning and in which it ultimately terminates. The Christ whom men must be led to know is Christ apprehended not in an empty vacuum but in the real context of the Church, the world and world history.

The Church has never deviated from the primitive kerygma. Christ is Christ, "yesterday and today and forever." His essential image—true God and true man—has never changed. The

Church can claim in truth that the faith which she has received from the Lord she has kept in all fidelity. But the preservation and transmission of this ancient faith have been heavy burdens which could not have been supported apart from the Spirit. For there are manifold factors that conspire against permanence in the midst of change. While the picture of Christ has not essentially deteriorated from its pristine image, the circumstances—the size, color and shape of the frame that enclose it—have changed. The result at times has been striking.

A careful comparison of the picture of Christ current in the popular piety of the late Middle Ages with the Christ-image of the early Church, brings out the character of the transformation that the centuries wrought. The divergence, however, between the ancient and the medieval is not away from orthodoxy towards heresy; nor are the aberrations in which this decline is expressed univocal and universal. They are, rather, well-defined trends which throw light on Catholic theology as lived and experienced by the people rather than as studied and expounded by the masters. Exceptions to the movement of ideas which is outlined here, can be cited. For though medieval theology was rich, diversified and original, it was, generally speaking, dogmatically pure. The reproach, therefore, is not with the sacred doctrine of the Middle Ages but rather with its representatives who were not always sufficiently discriminating in supervising the quality of the spiritual food on which their people were feeding. The pure Catholic faith which is contemplated by the theologian should also be purely transmitted to the people. For Christian doctrine, as a *corpus* of saving truth, is an indispensable food for the spiritual life of man.

The Christ-piety of the pre-Nicene Church centered about Christ in the context of liturgy and Bible. It was, therefore, liturgical and biblical in spirit and language. In stressing the mediatory and sacerdotal role of Christ in the worship of the community, it was led to emphasize His humanity. As Mediator, Christ reconciled man to God; and this reconciliation He effected by the sacrifice which He offered as Priest. These offices, Mediator and Priest, central to the saving work of Christ, are continued in the apostolic ministry of His Church. Both offices are rooted in the human nature, that same nature in which Christ lives as the Head of His Mystical Body.[2]

The primitive Church neither denied nor overlooked the divinity of Christ. This precious truth was fundamental to her faith. In the apostolic kerygma Christ is presented as God incarnate, herald of the Gospel, witness to the Father, raised from the death of the Cross, drawn up to heaven, enthroned at the right hand of the Father who has clothed Him in majesty, serenity and glory. From thence one day He is to come to judge the living and the dead. With correct balance the Pauline hymn (Phil. 2:5–11) portrays the parallel between the divine and the human in Christ:[3]

> Who, while he kept his character as God,
> did not consider his divine equality
> something to be proudly paraded.
>
> No, he despoiled himself,
> by taking on the Servant's character,
> becoming similar to mortal men.

And looking outwardly like any other man,
he carried self-abasement, through obedience,
right up to death, yes, death by the Cross.

Therefore did God in turn immediately exalt him
and graciously bestow on him the Name,
outweighing every other name,

that everyone, at Jesus' Name,
should bow adoring: those in heaven,
on earth, in the infernal regions,

and every tongue take up the cry,
"Jesus is Lord,"
thus glorifying God his Father.

According to these verses of St. Paul, the ultimate exaltation
of Christ involves both His humanity and divinity, His Incarnation and Redemption. "The man who accepted humiliation
of his own free will, is established at the very summit of creation, in the power and glory of God."[4]

The thanksgiving prayers in the *Didache,* one of the earliest
Christian writings (*ca.* 100–50) after the New Testament, show
how the primitive Church incorporated the Mediatorship of
Christ into her piety:[5]

Regarding the Eucharist. Give thanks as follows: First, concerning
the cup:

We give Thee thanks, Our Father, for the Holy Vine of David,

Thy Servant, which Thou hast made known to us through Jesus, Thy Servant.

To Thee be the glory for evermore.

Next, concerning the broken bread:

We give Thee thanks, Our Father, for the life and knowledge which Thou hast made known to us through Jesus, Thy Servant. To Thee be the glory for evermore.

The prayer-pattern is clear. The community ("we") offers its thanksgiving to God the Father through the ministry of Jesus as a service of mediation.

The Christ of the early Church was comprehended in biblical terms as the fulfillment of the prophets. In point of view, more paschal than incarnational, its attention was fixed on the Risen Christ, "the King of the ages, who is immortal, invisible, the one only God" (1 Tim. 1:17). "The suffering servant," "the lamb led to slaughter," died indeed, but He died as the Good Shepherd who gives his life that his sheep might live. Through His royal death on the Cross came the exaltation, honor and approbation of the resurrection. The crucifixion, therefore, was not an ignominy. It was a triumph—*regnavit a ligno Deus!*[6] For the early Church the Cross was a victory-symbol in which the absence of the *corpus* intimated the resurrection. Assumed into heaven as "the King of glory," Christ remains celestial mediator, the center of Christian life.[7] From here below the Church looks up to its Lord crowned with majesty and power and awaits with expectation His final return to His own.[8]

The Christology of the early Church developed under the influence of a number of different factors which are too complicated to be analyzed here. But in the one hundred and twenty-six years between the Councils of Nicaea (325) and Chalcedon (451), the major architectonic of Christ-piety took its definitive form. In answer to the anti-Trinitarianism of Arius, the Fathers of Nicaea defined the true divinity and natural sonship of the Logos, the presupposite of all true Christian piety. Later, the Council of Ephesus (431) entered more properly into the anthropology of Christ by specifying the oneness of His divine person which subsists in two natures, divine and human; and by defining the perfect maternity of Mary as Mother of God (*Theotokos*). The Council of Chalcedon further delineated the character of the relationship between the natures of the Incarnate Word of God. After their hypostatic union they remain perfect, distinct, unconfused and unconfounded. In the subsequent development of her doctrine the Church neither extenuated nor deviated from this dogmatic pattern of the early councils. That Christ is true God and true man remains basic to the Christian faith.

The Christological problem, inasmuch as it touches on Christian spirituality, arises not from a negation of this ancient conciliar faith, but rather from the undue emphasis and stress which the medieval Church placed on various aspects of it. Throughout the centuries the image of Christ has remained constant in itself; but the focus shifts in sharpness and clarity; light and shadow vary in intensity. The tendency of religious truths to be infected in their normal growth by extraneous matter is prevalent throughout the history of spirituality. And the Christianity of the Middle Ages was no exception to this tendency.

The transmission of the biblical, the patristic and the conciliar modes of conceiving Christ to the early medieval world was conditioned by the interplay of two influential factors, the racial and the theological, that is the Germanic and the Arian in contest with the Latin and the Catholic.[9] The barbarian peoples who entered Europe in the course of the late fifth and sixth centuries were passionately Semi-Arian. As spiritual children of Ulphilas (d. *ca.* 383), they essentially held, with the synods of Seleucia-Rimini (359), that the Son is so subordinate to the Father that He can be considered only a creature.[10] To refute this distortion of the confession of Nicaea was the task of the Catholic Church, especially in those areas under the influence of the Visigoths who were militant in their Semi-Arianism. In violent reaction against the teaching of these unorthodox barbarians the Church strongly and emphatically confessed its faith in the divinity of Christ. The whole polemic, lasting more than a century, resulted in the creation of new patterns of religious thought and expression which in time became commonplace in Catholic usage.

For example, in the ancient Catholic formula, *Per Christum Dominum nostrum* (through Christ our Lord) which expresses Christ's mediatorship in liturgical prayer, the Semi-Arians saw a clear attestation to the subordination of the Son to the Father. In fact, they so distorted the meaning of the formula that it became Arian in sense. The Catholic answer was to recast it in more explicit terms: *Per Dominum nostrum Iesum Christum Filium tuum qui tecum vivit et regnat in unitate Spiritus sancti, Deus* . . . (through Our Lord Jesus Christ, Thy Son, who with Thee lives and reigns in the unity of the Holy

Spirit, God . . .). Thus the divinity of the Son and His equality with the Father were confirmed by placing the two in perfect parallel. The same transforming influence is seen at work in the revision of the doxology. The ancient formula, *Gloria Patri per Filium cum Spiritus sancto*, which indicates the order of procession within the Godhead and relation of the persons to the economy of salvation—"Glory be to the Father through the Son with the Holy Spirit"—was altered to *Gloria Deo Patri et Filio et Spiritui sancto* (Glory be to God the Father and to the Son and to the Holy Spirit). Thereby the divinity, equality and trinity of the three persons were at one and the same time explicitly affirmed and confessed.

Both these new formulas are Trinitarian in their profession of the faith of Nicaea. Both are dogmatically pure and proper. But there is latent here a tendency which will have serious repercussions in the public prayer of the Church. If the divine person of Christ be so stressed in the formulation of prayer that His human nature falls more and more into shadow, then the offices of Christ, his Mediatorship, Priesthood and Headship, which depend on this human nature are also obscured. This involved for the character of liturgical prayer (and the prayer forms depending on it) a first-class displacement which increased as Christ was apprehended more from the Trinitarian than the Incarnational point of view.

This kind of thinking and speaking inevitably resulted in a pronounced Trinitarianism. There is nothing novel in the Church's profession of the *fides Trinitaria* which traces its origins back to the most ancient and reliable sources of Christianity and ultimately to Christ Himself. Novel is the medieval handling of the mystery. The dogma is thrust forward in such wise that the substance of the faith becomes identical with the doctrine of the Trinity.[11] As the divinity of the Logos, 'one of the Trinity,' is emphasized, the humanity is depressed. The simple formula which expresses this tendency, *Gloria Deo nostro Iesu Christo* (Glory to our God, Jesus Christ), is perfectly true but it does not sufficiently accent the incarnational aspect of the Christ-mystery. It tends, therefore, to distort the structure of the ancient kerygma in which it is *God made man* who is proclaimed the Saviour of the world.

In the old Roman liturgy the Three Persons are rarely mentioned explicitly. In fact, the word *Trinitas* occurs only twice in the Sacramentary of Verona (Leonine). More normal was the prayer to God the Father through Christ Jesus the Mediator. But in the Carolingian period Trinitarianism became a prominent element in liturgical prayer. From this time (*ca.* 800) stem prayers such as *Suscipe, sancta Trinitas* and *Placeat tibi, sancta Trinitas,* which are still to be found in the Roman Missal. The *Kyrie eleison,* originally a triple invocation to the Saviour as Lord (*Kyrie*) and Anointed (*Christe*), now becomes Trinitarian by a new interpretation; and the *Ter Sanctus* follows the same new path.[12] By the middle of the eighth century Trinitarian prefaces are in use; and about 800 the first complete Mass in honor of the Trinity, probably composed by Alcuin and intended as a Sunday votive Mass, appeared. By the year 1000 the Frankish Church was observing a special feast of the Trinity which Alexander III (d. 1181) declined to celebrate in Rome because he considered it superfluous. By the thirteenth century the Preface of the Trinity began to be the normal Sunday Preface; and in the following century (1334) Pope John XXII extended the feast of the Trinity to the universal Church.

As early as the beginning of the eighth century there are intimations of the transformation of Sunday into a Trinitarian day. For example, in the Irish *Antiphonary of Bangor* (680–91) a hymn of praise in honor of the Trinity is prescribed to be used on Sunday after the *Laudate pueri;*[13] and in another Irish work of a later date, Sunday, "the blessed day of the Lord," is hailed as the day on which creation began, the day of the nativity and resurrection of the Lord, also the day on which the Spirit descended upon the Church.[14] Of further significance in this gradual evolution is the revised text of the hymn used at Sunday Matins (from October to Lent, Advent and Christmas time excepted).[15] In the original text the Risen Christ, the Lord both of the old and the new creation, both of the old and the new Sabbath, is exalted as God and man. Under all aspects Sunday is His day. In the revision this concept is partly displaced in favor of the Trinity which created the world on the first day. In the course of the early Middle Ages Sunday continued to develop in a Trinitarian sense. Finally, the Sundays after the Paschal season came to be numbered either from Pentecost or from Trinity Sunday as their *terminus*. The day of the Risen Lord had become the day of the Blessed Trinity.

As Christology fell more and more under the spell of this Trinitarian movement, the center of gravity shifted sharply at the expense of the humanity of Christ; and with this important shift the central offices of Christ, His Priesthood and Mediatorship, fell into relative obscurity. The vacuum was gradually filled by Mary and the saints, who were introduced as special mediators between Christ and man. From the Carolingian period on, this movement is reflected in the diptychs and triptychs—artistic representations from the life of Mary and the saints—which dominate the altars; and, at the same time, the relics of the saints whose cult becomes ever more central, appear on the very altar-table where formerly only the sacred species were allowed to rest. Like the *oblata* and the Cross they too are incensed. The expansion of the *Sanctorale* throughout the year and the multiplication of special votive Masses to implore the intercession of the saints testify to the vigor of these undisciplined tendencies. The *Legenda aurea* of Jacob of Voragine (d. 1298) shows how incrusted in legend hagiography had become. Its fantastic presentation of the lives of the saints formed an open foyer to popular superstition. Unfortunately this kind of literature had a certain influence even on liturgical texts and piety.

The danger inherent in this movement of ideas was far deeper than these outward signs indicated. As the mediatorship of Christ was overshadowed by the intrusion of other less important factors, so was His priesthood. Thus, in liturgical worship Christ came in time to be looked upon more as the one who consecrates *for* the Church than as the one who sacrifices *with* it. In the exaltation of the divine nature in Christ over the human, in the depression of the latter in favor of the former, the character of the Word of God incarnate was drawn out of focus in popular piety. In these terms the sacred humanity tended to be looked upon as a kind of receptacle for the divine person, an instrument through which God dealt with man. In consequence, the earthly life, the human existence of the

Christ of history, took on the character of a theophany. Diminished in this mode of thought was the idea that Christ, as the Incarnate Logos, was true man, and as man played a decisive role in salvation and its historical development; that the human Christ, sacred by His indissoluble union with the Logos, was and is in His own right Priest, Prophet and King of the New Law; and that as man this same Christ now glorified and risen presides over the whole Church which is His Mystical Body.

The more His divinity came to the fore in Christ-piety, the more awesome and dreadful became the Eucharist as a sacrament. For here it was *God* who was received! Thus the faithful turned aside in fear and trembling before the Eucharist which in an earlier age of the Church had been accepted as the new manna from heaven graciously granted to God's chosen people. The trend here is bifurcated in direction: positively, in an exaggerated cultus of the Real Presence as God's Presence; and, negatively, in an almost total abstention from the Eucharist as transcending unworthy humanity.[16]

In the course of the late twelfth century the meaning of certain traditional words in the Catholic vocabulary shifted. The change is impressive and indicative of a trend. Thus, the ancient expressions, *corpus Christi* and *mysticum corpus,* took on new meanings. The latter, formerly used to designate the Eucharist, now came to be applied to the Church as the Mystical Body of Christ, while the former was reserved for the Sacrament of the Altar. But as the mystical headship of Christ which is rooted in His humanity faded, significant repercussions of this phenomenon were felt in the formulation of the concept of the Mystical Body.

The Church now assumed increasingly the character of an earthly society bound together by law into a hierarchy of ascending authority. The import of this development is reflected in the *De ecclesiastica potestate* of Giles of Rome (d. 1316)— one of the first treatises *De ecclesia*—whose concept of the Church is essentially an expression of the complexity of the legal relations (rights and obligations) over which the pope presides. In fact, in this period, the age of Boniface VIII (d. 1303), "the notion of *corpus mysticum* . . . served to describe the body politic, or *corpus iuridicum,* of the Church." In consequence, the headship of the pope, "the chief Prince moving and regulating the whole Christian polity," became more juridical in character.[17] This thinking, so very legal in its point of view, ultimately prepared the groundwork for that rigid juridicism and moralism which would come to flowering in the Church of the subsequent centuries. In view of this change in ecclesiastical thought it is interesting to note that the question could be raised at this time whether the Church could be better ruled by a pope who is a good lawyer or by one who is a good theologian.

But no Christian may neglect the humanity of Christ. It is a matter of evangelical faith that the Saviour was true man, "like unto us in all things save sin alone." And to this pivotal truth the medieval man was faithful. Generally speaking, when he thought of Christ in His human nature, he thought of the historical Christ, the Christ of the Gospels, the Christ of *then*. Psychologically he tried to reach back to the historical moment of the Gospel event, to project himself into it, to reproduce it imaginatively, to share in it. When the medieval man considered Christ as He is *now*, accent fell heavily on His divinity; when, however, he thought of Christ as man, he looked to *then*, to the distant historical past, to Christ as He appears in the Gospel.

In the primitive Church as it is known in the historical sources the Resurrection-theme was paramount. The object of her faith was the Risen Christ, Jesus Christ, true God and true man, who is *now* enthroned in majesty and glory. In the medieval Church the themes of the Incarnation and the Passion, as historical mysteries, occupy the first place in its consideration of the sacred humanity of *Christus secundum carnem*.[18] This appears unmistakably in the external expression of its religious art and literature, its liturgy and spirituality.

From the solemn definition of the Council of Ephesus in 431 that Mary was indeed the *Theotokos*, God's true Mother, stems the great Marian movement in the Western Church. The development, heightened under the increasing stress which was placed on the divine element in Christ, unfolded artistically, theologically and spiritually as an Incarnational theme. Within the liturgical year there emerged in parallel with the Paschal cycle (Lent-Easter) an Incarnational cycle (Advent-Christmas), and within this new annual cycle the feast of the Annunciation was soon (*ca.* 430) fixed on March 25th as a pivot to Christmas on December 25th. Around these two new solemnities a cluster of Marian (Incarnational) feasts grew in the course of time with an ever present inclination to invade the Paschal (Sunday) cycle. By the fifth century Christmas-Epiphany had acquired a season of preparation, Advent, which gradually lost its eschatological character in favor of an historical commemoration. The four weeks of Advent were conceived as representing the four thousand Old Testament years leading to the birth of Christ. Advent-Epiphany paralleled Lent-Easter. Both terminated in a baptismal festival.

The introduction of the Incarnational cycle into the liturgy is in harmony with its inner character. For the Incarnation as a Christian mystery is in the heart of salvation history which the liturgy reflects. In the course of its historical development this new cycle tended to overtake the old Resurrection cycle, to displace in the minds of the faithful the solemnity of the Risen Christ from its central place, and to obscure the Paschal-theme, the core of all Christian mysteries. But this inclination perfectly harmonized with the medieval propensity for commemorating the historical Christ of *then*.

From the very beginning of Christianity Sunday was the Lord's Day. Beside it Saturday grew as Mary's special day.[19] And to honor this weekly observance Alcuin (d. 804) composed two Masses, *De beata Maria*. Early medieval Mariology stood on the patristic tradition; but it developed this heritage in a characteristic way. Whereas for the Latin Fathers the parallels, Eve-Mary and Mary-Church, were valuable for their universal, objective and typical significance within the broad framework of salvation history, the Carolingians interpreted them in terms of the present, the actual and the personal. Mary was exalted as mediatrix, intercessor, the solitary cell from which the whole Church grows, its member par excellence. In the patristic period the gaze of the faithful turned from Mary (God's Mother) to Christ (God's Son) with a maximum consideration of the latter. The divine maternity was not applied as a measure defining the personal character of Mary. In the Carolingian period the Mother of Christ in her individual, personal attributes entered more prominently into the foreground. Now religious thought focused on Mary as such. The movement of thought was from Christ to Mary and the light of His mystery was now fully turned on the figure of Mary.[20]

In the period between the beginning of the ninth century and the end of the Middle Ages, especially between the times of St. Peter Damiani (d. 1072) and St. Bernard (d. 1153), devotion to Mary developed into an integral part of religious life. The very rich heritage of Marian hymns, poetry, prayers, churches and art works that has come down from this period attests to the vigor of this development as clearly as any dogmatic pronouncement or theological treatise. Characteristic at this time (twelfth century) is the shift in the exegetical interpretation of the *Canticle of Canticles* from an ecclesiological to a Marian sense.[21] Mary enters more and more into the center of private prayer, as her mediatorship between Christ and man is accented. And because this intercessory office is viewed as resting on her title *Theotokos,* the maternity theme dominates both art and piety. Mary conceived Jesus by the power of the Holy Spirit. She begot Him and mothered Him. He is the infant who reposes on her knees before her bosom. Mother and Child, inseparable both in prayer and in art, stand together. He, who had no mother in heaven, has no father on earth. Mary and Jesus are reciprocal parts of one theme—Incarnation. Insistence on this way of looking at the divine maternity leads directly to Christ-child piety, a devotion thoroughly consonant with the medieval mode of contemplating the historical Christ of *then.* Here the Saviour, who is *now* the Risen Lord, is regarded as if He were *now* "the child wrapped in swaddling clothes and lying in a manger." Dominant are the histories of Bethlehem and Nazareth.

While medieval piety concentrated on the Incarnation, especially on the opening hours of the Saviour's earthly life, it did not overlook the Passion, the conclusion of His existence on earth. For in this matter the medieval Church was heir to a venerable tradition reaching back to the Fathers of the Church. In the *Carmina Natalicia* of St. Paulinus of Nola (d. 431), who wrote his praise of the Cross to honor St. Felix, we see the best aspects of this early tradition:[22]

> O Cross, sign of God's great affection,
>> heaven's glory, men's eternal salvation,
>> terror of the wicked, strength of the just,
>> light of the faithful . . .
> You are men's link with Christ, the Mediator:
> You brought them peace through the covenant
>> made on you.
> You are man's ladder, whereby he may climb
>> into heaven.

And in the following century Venantius Fortunatus (d. *ca.* 600), 'the last of the Roman poets,' set forth the glory and the majesty of the Cross in his well-known Passion hymn:[23]

> Vexilla regis prodeunt,
> Fulget crucis mysterium,
> Quo carne carnis conditor
> Suspensus est patibulo.

Impleta sunt quae concinit
David fideli carmine,
Dicendo nationibus:
"Regnavit a ligno Deus."

Its conclusion, "O crux, ave, spes unica," re-echoes the hope
which redeemed humanity finds in the Cross.

Medieval piety which found its inspiration and center in the
Passion and the Cross was too often infected with excessive
subjectivism. Its approach was historical, detailed, sympathetic
and sentimental. The faithful are called back to that dread hour
of the mystery of the Passion; and, overpowered with tender
compassion before the bitter physical torment of the Lord—
now exaggerated and distorted out of due proportion—they
are invited to re-experience in imagination His physical and
mental suffering. The Passion of Christ becomes almost an
end in itself, too often unrelated to the glorious resurrection
and ascension, the inevitable conclusion of the Passion-narrative and the mysteries in whose light alone the *beata Passio*
becomes meaningful.

The Passion-theme is one of the most prominent themes in
medieval art. Its ultimate origin is the Gospel and its center is
the Cross. The crucifix was unknown to the primitive Church;
its Passion-symbol was the simple Cross—or the Christos-
monogram—as a sign that the Lord, who died, still lives. Typical of the religious spirit which enlivened the Passion-art of
Late Antiquity are the mosaics and the arch of St. Apollinare
in Classe consecrated at Ravenna in 549. In the center is the
jeweled Cross of Christ; at either end stand *Alpha* and *Omega*;

above it the symbolic ICHTHUS (Fish: 'Jesus Christ, Son of God, Saviour'); and below *Salus Mundi,* 'the salvation of the world.' At the apex is *Christos.* The figures of Moses and Elias, and SS. Peter, James and John represented as lambs, recall the mystery of the Transfiguration, while salvation history is intimated by the symbols—the angel, the lion, the ox and the eagle —of the four evangelists. The peace, serenity and victory of the Resurrection are suggested by the procession of the innocent white lambs who stand about this Cross of glory on which their Good Shepherd conquered.[24]

In the course of the sixth and seventh centuries the crucifix was introduced into Italy and Spain from the East (Syria). Before that date it was unknown in the West. From the eleventh century onward it became customary to place a crucifix on the altar-table; by the twelfth it dominated the wall behind the altar. The early Romanesque crucifixes idealize the suffering Christ. In representing Him as priest and king reigning from the Cross, they try to bring out the ultimate theological meaning of the mystery of the redemptive death. Thus, for example, in a bronze crucifix from Werden in Germany, dating from about the year 1060 (from the Ottonian period, therefore), we behold the Christ of majesty in serene repose. The Cross is His throne of glory. His head is not crowned with thorns nor is His face suffused with agony. He is indeed the suffering Christ who has fallen into that slumber from which He will soon awake to glory.[25]

The manuscript art of these centuries witnessed a development which parallels that of the plastic arts. At a date as early as the Sacramentary of Gellone (770) the *T* of the *Te igitur* of the Canon of the Mass is embellished into a Cross. By the eleventh century the Cross has become independent and occupies the facing page. The earliest representations are full of splendor and glory. The colors gold, blue and red dominate. Biblical typology finds expression in the sacrifices of Abel, Melchisedech and Abraham. In an *Evangeliarium* (*ca.* 1050) from Echternach we see the Crucified in majesty, vested as a priest in royal purple, with a nimbus of glory surrounding His sacred head; into a chalice flows His saving blood (Eucharistic-theme); the serpent (Satan) and Adam and Eve stand in awe face to face with the Crucified (Redemption-theme); Mary and John (Ecclesial-theme) watch in reverent silence; the sun and moon (Majesty-theme) shroud their faces before the spectacle of the dying Saviour. The whole representation is at once both religious and theological in that it brings out the ultimate significance of the Gospel mystery in terms of salvation history.[26]

With time this kind of artistic interpretation, inspired by theological considerations, changed toward realism and naturalism. Restraint is dropped. The final moments of the Passion come into ever greater prominence, while the redemptive significance of the historical event sinks behind 'the hill of the skull.' The suffering Christ appears conquered by the most dismal aspects of pain and death, and this way of conceiving the Passion vividly reflects the macabre spirit which pervaded the religious life of the late medieval world. Probably the most striking example of the Passion-art of this period is the celebrated *retable* of Isenheim, the work of Mathias Grünewald (d. 1528). Here the crucified Christ who hangs on the Cross in the darkness of Calvary is the very incarnation of that despair which many late medieval theologians discovered in the words: "My God, my God, why hast Thou forsaken me?"[27] The whole portrayal breathes forth a dismal agony which seems out of harmony with the full import of the Passion-narrative.

It was by means of the cruel realism of this art that the faithful were introduced to Jesus as a man of sorrows and despair, without hope, without solace. In the tenth century the first artistic representations of the scourging at the pillar appear; and soon other Passion-scenes (for example, the crowning with thorns) become common, always portrayed with tender compassion and increasing naturalism. The death-event of Christ is treated almost as the terminal moment of sorrow, anguish and suffering. It is not surprising that the late Middle Ages witnessed the development of the cult of the dead Christ which found artistic expression in a variety of forms often grotesquely realistic.[28] The age teemed with the death-image, and it was inevitable that this morbid tension would make its way into religion. In view of the fact that this religious art came to its fullness in the last phase of the Middle Ages—on the eve of the Reformation—one might well ponder whether the suffering which is reflected in the face of the crucified Christ is not indeed an expression of the *Angst* of His Mystical Body on earth, the *ecclesia reformanda*.

The Passion-theme filled the religious life of the Middle Ages. In the second half of the seventh century the feasts in honor of the Holy Cross—its *Exaltation,* on September 14th and its *Finding,* on May 3rd—were introduced. Later Alcuin gave new stimulus to the cult of the Cross by the votive Mass

De cruce, which he composed in its honor, and by the series of prayers to the crucified Christ which he prepared.[29] The Sign of the Cross came more and more into popular usage and, as we shall see, the relics connected with the Passion entered into greater prominence in the religious life of the people. In the late Middle Ages the Passion-play, influenced by the liturgical veneration of the Cross on Good Friday, became popular. And here the people could witness the vividly moving drama of the suffering and the dying Saviour, re-enacted with much music, song, color and all the theatrical appurtenances of religious pageantry.

Perhaps most significant of the character of the influence of the Passion on monastic life was the introduction of the corporal discipline, the bodily, self-inflicted penance, into religious observance. This was largely the work of the reformer St. Peter Damiani (d. 1072) who made every effort to inculcate this novel practice in the various monasteries with which he was affiliated.[30] By the end of the Middle Ages this voluntary, penitential self-discipline, a practice totally unknown to the ancient Church, had become common to almost all religious orders. It is hard to exaggerate the consequences which this rigorous asceticism worked on the development of the spiritual life.[31]

Christ-piety centering around the suffering Jesus was fundamental to the spiritual doctrine of the two most distinguished religious leaders of the medieval world: St. Bernard of Clairvaux (d. 1153) and St. Francis of Assisi (d. 1226). Both are noted in the history of Christian spirituality for their insistence on the true following of Christ and for their appreciation of His sacred humanity. Their picture of Christ is essentially and primarily that of the historical Christ, as He once was on earth, rather than of the glorious Christ, as He now is in heaven. In the middle of their spiritual perception of the divine economy stands the Incarnate Word of God in the precise historical circumstances in which He manifested Himself in this life. Central were the questions: How did Jesus become man? What did He do on earth? How did He suffer and die? To meditate on these points with tender affection and total abandonment was the royal road of sanctity. It overflowed into imitation of Christ. Preoccupied with the life and death of their Saviour, these spiritual masters tended to leave the mystery of the Resurrection-Ascension in the background.

In his twenty-second sermon on the *Canticle of Canticles* St. Bernard states his position this way:[32]

> But now in this life I am not allowed either to behold or to study Christ (I do not say this without tears) as the king seated in glory above the Cherubim, seated on the high and mighty throne, in that form in which, equal to the Father, he was begotten before the day star in the splendor of the saints, in which the angels desire without cease to behold him, God in God. I as a man speak of him as a man to men according to that form in which . . . he is less than the angels . . . I speak of him as gentle rather than sublime, and as anointed, not mighty. In a word, I speak of him whom the Spirit of the Lord anointed, and sent to preach the Gospel to the poor, to heal the contrite of heart, preach pardon to the captives and freedom to the confined, to preach the acceptable year of the Lord.

Obviously in this approach to the Gospel the Resurrection and the Ascension, as mysteries involving the present King of glory, stand very much in the inaccessible background.

The stigmata which the poor St. Francis received on Mt. Alvernia in September 1224 vividly symbolize Franciscan spirituality. It was an expression of his "resolve to observe the Holy Gospel in all things and through all things."[33] For now 'stigmatized,' he was placed in both spiritual and physical parallel with the wounded Christ with whom he wished to live and suffer in evangelical poverty. This mystical experience, the culmination of a life devoted to the Passion, found its ultimate inspiration in the Crucified. "For, Francis, while deep in prayer before the crucifix, heard the Lord speak to him and call him by name: 'Francis, go, build up my house which, as you see, is in total decay!' "[34] His whole religious life was an expression of devotion to the Cross. In the *Legenda maior* St. Bonaventure sums up his career in these terms:[35]

The great and wondrous mystery of the Cross . . . was so fully revealed to this child of Christ that his whole life consisted in following only the footsteps of the Cross, in drinking only the sweetness of the Cross, in preaching only the glory of the Cross.

The mystical encounter of Francis and Christ on the heights of Mt. Alvernia, this "miracle of love which astonished Europe," gave rise to all kinds of new sensible forms of art and piety which centered in the Crucified. Under the influence of the saint a distinctive religious tradition grew up among his followers, and through them Passion-spirituality became popular throughout Europe in a way unknown up to that time.

The Passion-piety of the late Middle Ages expressed itself in a number of devotions which concentrated on different aspects of the suffering Christ. Perhaps the most popular and beloved was the *Via Crucis,* the so-called Stations of the Cross. Here in fourteen tableaux were represented the principal scenes of the Passion, generally commencing with the condemnation of Jesus by Pilate and terminating in His burial by Joseph of Arimathea. Certain prayers and hymns were specified to be used in connection with each station. The whole spirit of this prayer-form was colored by profound sadness for and sympathy with the suffering Christ. As a devotion it was admirably conceived. It was simple, direct and impressive. It was biblical, too, at least to an extent. But the stark realism of the artistic representations often tended to overemphasize the physical aspects of the *Via Crucis;* and by concluding the series of meditations with the burial of the dead Jesus a note of finality was struck that was out of harmony with the deepest meaning of the Passion-narrative. The *Via Crucis* appeared as a mystery contained in itself. And by its insistence on the historical it carried the faithful back to Calvary, to Jesus suffering *then,* rather than lifting them upward in spirit to Jesus *now* in glory who, having suffered once at the hands of men, suffers no more.

Medieval devotion to the Passion expressed itself in a variety of concrete forms. Its object, at first the mystery of the suffering Christ, soon passed to special aspects of this mystery, for example to the Five Wounds and to the Precious Blood. Both devotions can be justified on the basis of dogma and theology. They are not, therefore, negligible factors in Christ-piety. The Risen Saviour remains marked with the Wounds, the visible signs of His suffering and death; and the Eucharist contains His Blood which the Christian must drink in order to live that

life which he has received from his Lord. But in fostering
these devotions the simple people often lacked the necessary
finesse. At times the tendency is present to separate the sacred
Wounds and the Precious Blood from the totality of the humanity of Christ by cultivating them as if they were ends in
themselves. Then, too, both of these devotions were open to
the infection, so rampant in medieval religion, of superstition.
Thus, 28,430 drops of sacred Blood were reputed to have been
shed by Christ in the Passion; and 5,466 (or 5,475) wounds to
have been inflicted on His Body. St. Gertrude (d. *ca.* 1301–02)
was accustomed every day to say an aspiration in honor of each
of these more than five thousand wounds.[36]

The medieval world had intense devotion to the relics of
the Passion—the True Cross, the crown of thorns, the nails,
the sacred lance, the veil of Veronica, the winding sheet, the
sacred tears of Christ, and the Precious Blood.[37] Masses in
honor of the Passion, the relics of the Passion, and the suffering
Christ, for example His face and His soul, came into common
use in the fourteenth century. These were significant factors
in the spiritual life of that day. In fact, the importance of the
devotion to the Wounds of Christ can be measured from the
incredible efficacy which was popularly ascribed to the *Missa
de quinque vulneribus Christi*. According to legend the text
of this Mass was originally composed by St. John the Evan-
gelist and later revealed by an angel to Pope Boniface II (530–
32) under marvelous circumstances. In the popular imagination its power was fabulous. For "whenever any priest should
devoutly read this Mass for the sick, either for himself or another, there is a recovery of health, and in the future life

eternal; and a man in straitened circumstances will find release in this world."[38]

At times the language in which these pious devotions were expressed was sharply vivid, highly imaginative even to the point of excessive realism. In the *Philomena*—a lyric almost technically perfect in form, personal in emotion, "filled with the new inspiration which was the secret of the gospel of Assisi"—John Pecham (d. 1292), the Franciscan Archbishop of Canterbury, sings of "the sweet bath" in the Blood of Christ in which the just soul is laved.[39] And in the *Anima Christi,* an early fourteenth-century prayer commonly but erroneously ascribed to St. Ignatius Loyola, we read:

> Blood of Christ, inebriate me.
> Water of the side of Christ, wash me.
> . . .
> Within your wounds hide me.
> . . .

The basic concepts, salvation through the Blood and the Wounds of Christ, are evangelical, but the figurative language in which they are cast by the poet is overdeveloped in the realism of its imagery.

From the middle of the twelfth century onward sentimentality, as an emotional, sensible, affective response to Jesus, takes hold of Christ-piety. This appears especially in the medieval comprehension of 'Jesus as Mother.'[40] In the *Pagina Meditationum* of Margaret of Oyngt (d. 1310), prioress at Poleteins near Lyons, the maternity of Christ appears in these terms:[41]

Are you not, Christ, my Mother and more than a mother? The mother, who bore me, knew the pains of labor perhaps through a day and a night. But, beautiful, sweet Lord, on my account . . . you have labored thirty years. Ah, beautiful, sweet Lord, how bitterly you labored for me, all my life. But when the time came in which you had to beget me, so great was your labor that your holy sweat was like drops of blood which rushed over your body and down to the ground.

And, later, Julian of Norwich (d. *ca.* 1413) in *The Sixteen Revelations of Divine Love* discusses the Trinity from the point of view of these three properties: paternity, maternity and sovereignty. She speaks of Jesus—"our Mother by mercy"—in these terms:[42]

Jesus is our true Mother. To him we owe our existence—the first condition of all maternity—and our conservation with a tenderness of love which is endlessly renewed. God is our Mother as truly as He is our Father . . . Jesus is our true Mother . . . in virtue of our creation, and our true Mother by grace in consequence of the Incarnation. All the beautiful functions and the sweet duties of maternity belong to the second Person.

Tied in with sentimentality in Christ-piety is the notion of 'sweetness'—the sweet Jesus—which flavors the atmosphere of private prayer. This mode of religious thought, so beloved in the Burgundian circle of St. Bernard, found noble expression in the *Dulcis Iesu memoria,* a poem originating in the milieu of the English Cistercians of the early twelfth century.[43] Here there is question of "the memory of the sweet Jesus," who, sweet "above honey and all else," is "the true sweetness of the heart." The imagery throughout the poem is dominated by the ardent, vividly warm language of mystical love. The already mentioned *Philomena* presents the mystical day of the nightingale—a type of the just soul—which dies in an ecstasy of burning love and tender sympathy as the circle of the hours reaches the ninth point, the moment of *Consummatum est.* It is death from sheer compassion with the Crucified.[44] In the author's conception of the Christian's love of Christ the relationship of lover to beloved is expressed in artificial, unreal, conflated terms, perhaps even influenced by the spirit of courtly love. It is essentially an allegory, an artistic work, whose inspiration arises from a realistic confrontation with the history of the Passion. It looks, therefore, at the Crucified more as now suffering and dying than as now rising and living.

But at the same time another tone, more rigorous in the texture of its thought and expression than that of 'the sweet Jesus,' can be recognized in the spirituality of the late Middle Ages. The *Dies irae,* probably the work of Thomas of Celano, introduces us to the medieval God of righteousness and justice, "the just judge of vengeance," before whose tribunal all the world will tremble in awe and terror. For in that dread moment, when the Lord comes to judge mankind, when the Book of Doom is to be brought forth, not even the just man will feel secure. It is the hour of inexorable decision, when the fate of humanity will hang in balance. Considerations such as these kept the medieval man in a state of constant nervous tension of fear mixed with hope. Face to face with death and judgment he quaked. For prominent in his thinking about the last things was "the written book" from whose pages the judgment of all would be read.

In both the art and the spirituality of the high Middle Ages two modes of representing Christ can be distinguished: the serene, majestic Christ, the Lord of revelation, the bringer of "grace and truth," such as He is depicted on the Royal Porch of Chartres; and the Christ, the judge of all men, the giver of the law, at whose feet stands humanity definitively judged— rewarded or condemned—the just called to heaven, the wicked consigned to hell. This Christ can only be placated by Mary, His loving Mother and our saving Mediatrix. For He is the stern judge who will examine with rigor both the living and the dead. On that dread day so intolerable for the wicked, that day of wrath and woe, when the world will melt away, it will be Mary alone who will be able to persuade the angry judge to turn His wrath away from mankind. That Mary is the only true *Mater Misericordiae* was the firm conviction of the late Middle Ages.[45]

In the tympanum art of the twelfth century, for example at La Lande-de-Cubzac (Girone), the inspiration of the Apocalypse (1:12–17) is in evidence as its thematic basis.[46] For in the first of the visions which St. John beheld at Patmos he saw "one like to a son of man . . . out of his mouth came forth a sharp two-edged sword; and his countenance was like the sun shining in its power." The late medieval representations of this theme stress the majesty of the tremendous king who is to sit in judgment on all humanity. In the Last Judgment of Roger de la Pasture (van der Weyden, *ca.* 1450) Christ the judge is depicted with the lily and the blessed at His right ear, the sword

and the damned at His left. For He is the Lord both of mercy
and of justice. But the progressive tendency is to accent the
sword that signifies justice.[47]

This kind of art, interlaced on all sides both by the Dance of
Death and by the Art of Dying, was to be found with increasing frequency as the late Middle Ages entered its autumn time.
In 1493 Hartmann Schedel brought out his world-history, *Das
Buch der Chroniken,* in which the final engraving is the Last
Judgment, presented of course in the traditional mode: Christ
sitting in judgment on the totality of mankind, part of which
(the just) is saved, part (the wicked) lost. Here we see the
decisive moment when man enters the realm either of light
and the angels or of darkness and the demons. Here again the
justice and the mercy of the Lord are symbolized by the sword
and the lily. Here again Mary stands forth as the intercessor
between Christ and man. "Luther had seen such pictures as
these and testified that he was utterly terror-stricken at the
sight of Christ the Judge."[48]

In a work entitled *Exhortation to all the Clergy Assembled
at Augsburg* (1530) which has been characterized as "a sum-
mary of all Lutheranism," Luther expressed his mind on the
Christ which he had come to know in the tradition of his day:[49]

The monks . . . depicted to all the world that holy and noble
woman, the virgin Mary, as a mediator for poor sinners, even for
her Son, Christ himself. For we all know, and I was as deep in it
as all the rest, that we were plainly taught to hold Mary in
Christ's place and office. We held Christ to be our angry judge and
Mary to be our throne of grace, where all our comfort and refuge

lay, if we did not wish to despair. Was that not a horrible innovation? Where were the bishops who rebuked such new blasphemers and betrayers of Christ who took away Christ's office and gave it to Mary, who taught us to flee from Christ and fear him as a whipmaster, and directed elsewhere our confidence which we owe to him as the true divine service? We have learned nothing but idolatry from these traitors!

However much these words strike us as an indignant exaggeration, there remains an element of truth in them. Without presenting the whole picture of the Christ of medieval piety, they do suggest a significant aspect of it, an area of reform which the Fathers of Trent overlooked, doubtlessly because they were too intimately affiliated with the Middle Ages to appreciate objectively the character of its piety.

It is almost impossible to determine the point at which popular Catholic piety turned from the late medieval concept of Christ. Certainly the development of the devotion to the Sacred Heart by St. John Eudes (d. 1680) and St. Margaret Mary (d. 1690) was decisive in many respects. For in this devotion which centered about the Heart of Jesus as a symbol of love the faithful were confronted with Christ in His human nature, now no longer the stern judge of mankind but the fathomless fountain of love. Christ was indeed the giver of gifts, but the first gift that He gave to men was His own love; and through this love all other gifts flowed. The inner spirit of the devotion aimed at Christian peace, confidence, hope, and release from overpowering fear and moral tension. The faithful were reminded once again that there was free, direct access to their Saviour as to one whose love for mankind far outstripped all else. In light of these considerations one no longer needed to draw back from the Eucharist in dread. Obviously this way of looking at the character of the God-man in the economy of salvation formed an effective antidote against both the stern legalism of the Middle Ages and the severe moralism of Jansenism.

But even this sublime conception of devotion to Christ experienced the infection of historical development. The most vivid representation of this distortion is embodied in the highly sentimental art which sprung up about the devotion. Here the interplay of idealism and realism is striking. The visage of Christ is portrayed with a delicacy and refinement that become almost offensive; His Heart, at times represented apart from His humanity, is shown as an anatomical organ surrounded with bright flames and crowned with sharp thorns. Love is symbolized by the heart; its intensity by flames. At the same time the element of impetration comes to the fore. For in the popular mind salvation can be securely attained by 'making the nine first Fridays.' And with the increased emphasis on reparation to the Sacred Heart the pure generosity of the love of Christ for all men seems to be diluted in the sense that this altruistic love must be repaid by reparation. With the rise of devotion to the Sacred Heart of Mary the inference began to develop that a new mediator must stand between humanity and Christ Jesus revealed in the fullness of His own sacred humanity.

Father Josef Jungmann's[50] evaluation of the piety of the Middle Ages as a period which witnessed "the almost total disappearance of the thought of Christ as Mediator," is with certain qualifications true of the whole long period between the Council of Trent and our own day. Piety both private and liturgical has not been Christo-centric in the specifically biblical sense. For various reasons which are too complex to explain here the Church did not probe this area of her spiritual doctrine with a view to the renewal and restoration of the image of Christ according to the simple, pure lines in which He revealed Himself.

The past twenty years have indeed witnessed a revolution in our way of conceiving Christ. New appreciation is given now to the role of His humanity in salvation and in the history of salvation. The encyclical *Mystici Corporis* (June 29, 1943) of Pius XII has drawn the attention of the Church once again to the close mystical relationship between the sacred humanity of Christ and the redeemed humanity of His faithful on earth. He is the Head; we are the members. Both have the same human nature. For "Christ not only took our nature, He became one of our flesh and blood with a frail body that could suffer and die . . . The only begotten Son of the Eternal Father wished to be a Son of Man that we might be made conformed to the image of the Son of God and be renewed according to the image of him who created us." This was indeed a saving message to a world in the tight bonds of universal war. And, later, in the encyclical *Mediator Dei* (November 20, 1947), the same pope explained to the Church the relation of Christ to worship of God. He is the "Mediator," wrote the pope, "between God and man, the High Priest who has gone before us into heaven, Jesus the Son of God . . . He has so willed that the priestly life begun with the supplication and sacrifice of his mortal

body should continue without intermission down the ages in his Mystical Body which is the Church."

The Vatican Constitution has aptly epitomized the role of Jesus Christ in Catholic spirituality:

God . . . when the fullness of time had come sent his Son, the Word made flesh . . . the Mediator between God and man. For his humanity, united with the person of the Word, was the instrument of our salvation. Therefore, in Christ "the perfect achievement of our reconciliation came forth and the fullness of divine worship was given to us."

NOTES

[1] Cf. St. Ambrose, *Epist.* 3, 4: "There we find with the Sacred Scripture, which contains the doctrine of eternal wisdom, the holy tabernacle wherein Christ dwells, who speaks to us and in whom we possess all."

[2] Cf. Pius XII's *Mystici Corporis* (June 29, 1943), a document admirable for its appreciation of the humanity of Christ: "The mystical Head, which is Christ, and the Church, which in this world like 'another Christ' bears his person, constitute one man in whom heaven and earth are joined in continuing the salutary work of the Cross."

[3] Cf. D. M. Stanley, S.J., "The Divinity of Christ in Hymns of the New Testament," *Proceedings of the Fourth Annual Meeting of the Society of Catholic College Teachers of Sacred Doctrine* (Notre Dame 1958), p. 21.

[4] Cf. F. X. Durrwell, C.SS.R., *The Resurrection* (New York 1960), p. 114.

[5] J. A. Kleist, S.J., tr., *The Didache,* Ancient Christian Writers 6 (Westminster 1948), p. 20.

[6] 'God has reigned from the tree,' obviously of the Cross. Cf. on the Cross in Passion-piety R. E. McNally, S.J., "Beata Passio," *Worship* 38 (1964), pp. 120–25.

[7] Cf. St. Ambrose, *De virginitate* 96: "All things we have in Christ . . . for us Christ is all. . . ."

[8] The eschatological spirit of the primitive Church is neatly epitomized in the expressed wishes: "Come, Lord Jesus!" (Apoc. 22:20) and *Marana tha,* "Lord, come!" (*Didache* 6).

[9] For the lines of development which I have followed here I am deeply indebted to J. Jungmann's, S.J., "Die Abwehr des Germanischen Arianismus und der Umbruch der religiösen Kultur im Frühen Mittelalter," *Liturgische Erbe und Pastorale Gegenwart* (Innsbruck 1960), pp. 3–86. It is poorly translated in *Pastoral Liturgy* (New York 1962), pp. 1–63.

[10] The Creed of Rimini in confessing that the Son is *"like to* his Father according to the Scriptures" showed its sympathy for Arianism.

[11] J. Jungmann, S.J., in *Pastoral Liturgy,* p. 34.

[12] J. Jungmann, S.J., *The Mass of the Roman Rite,* Vol. 2, p. 134.

[13] F. E. Warren, ed., *The Antiphonary of Bangor* 2 (London 1895), p. 32. Early Christian Ireland was under the strong influence of Visigothic Spain.

[14] R. E. McNally, S.J., " 'Dies Dominica': Two Hiberno-Latin Texts," *Mediaeval Studies* 22 (1960), pp. 355–61.

[15] J. Connelly, *Hymns of the Roman Liturgy* (Westminster 1957), pp. 4–5.

[16] This theme is treated more fully in Chapter IV.

[17] E. H. Kantorowicz, *The King's Two Bodies* (Princeton 1957), p. 206.

[18] The phrase, *Christus secundum carnem,* signifying Christ in his earthly life in the flesh—in contrast to *Christus secundum spiritum,* the Risen Christ in glory—is Pauline (2 Cor. 5:16).

[19] Cf. L. Gougaud, *Devotional and Ascetic Practises in the Middle Ages* (London 1927), pp. 66 ff., for the five traditional reasons for honoring Mary on Saturday.

[20] Cf. L. Scheffczyk, *Das Mariengeheimnis in Frömmigkeit und Lehre der Karolingerzeit* (Leipzig 1959), pp. 498–500.

[21] William of Newburgh (d. *ca.* 1199) in his *Explanatio Sacri Epithalamii in Matrem Sponsi* (ed., J. C. Gorman in *Spicilegium Friburgense* 6, [Freibourg 1960], p. 75) explains the Marian sense this way: "This is not the *Canticle of Canticles* which Mary sings with virgins or with mothers, but that truly is the *Canticle of Canticles* which she alone among mothers sings, and alone sings among virgins. For among mothers she sings a canticle of virginity, among virgins a canticle of maternity."

[22] A. Hamman, *Early Christian Prayers,* p. 204.

[23] Cf. J. Connelly, *op. cit.,* pp. 80–82. This hymn has also been described as "one of the first creations of purely medieval religious feeling." Cf. F. J. E. Raby, *A History of Christian Latin Poetry* (Oxford 1953), p. 89.

24 C. R. Morey, *Early Christian Art* (Princeton 1953), p. 290, plate 183.

25 H. Jantzen, *Ottonische Kunst* (Munich 1947), pp. 116–117.

26 W. Dirks, *Christi Passion* (Hamberg 1956), plate 11.

27 P. Schmitt, *Le retable d'Isenheim,* Orbis pictus 26 (Lausanne).

28 This is most vividly seen in the art, statuary, prayers, hymns, poetry, devotional books, sermons and acts of piety. The Passion-theme is not only present in the late Middle Ages, it dominates religious life.

29 G. Ellard, S.J., *Master Alcuin, Liturgist* (Chicago 1956), pp. 167–68.

30 The adversaries of the Saint reproached him for introducing this novel penance: "You wish to introduce a penance of a new kind, a penance which has remained unknown for so many centuries." Cf. L. Gougaud, O.S.B., *op. cit.,* pp. 186–87.

31 It is of significant note that St. Ignatius of Loyola in founding his Society at the end of the Middle Ages prescribed "no regular penances or corporal austerities obligatory on all."

32 *Sermo* 22, 3 (*PL* 183, 379AC).

33 *Vita Prima* 1, 30, 84, ed., *Analecta Franciscana* 10 (Florence 1926–41), p. 63.

34 *Vita Secunda* 1, 6, 10, ed., *ibid.,* p. 137.

35 *Legenda Maior, Miracula* 10, 8, ed., *ibid.,* p. 651.

36 A. Franz, *Die Messe im Deutschen Mittelalter,* p. 156.

37 *Ibid.,* pp. 157 ff.

38 *Ibid.,* p. 158. Pope Boniface, sick unto death, was told by the angel to rise . . . recite the Mass five times and he would regain his health.

39 F. J. E. Raby, *op. cit.,* pp. 426, 428.

40 Cf. A. Cabassut, O.S.B., "Une dévotion médiévale peu connue. La dévotion à Jésus notre Mère," *Revue d'Ascétique et de Mystique* 25 (1949), pp. 234–45.

41 *Ibid.,* p. 240.

42 *Ibid.,* p. 241.

43 Cf. A. Wilmart, O.S.B., "Le 'Jubilus' dit de Saint Bernard," *Ephemerides liturgicae* (1943), pp. 2–285.

44 Cf. F. J. E. Raby, *op. cit.,* p. 427. Compassion for Mary parallels compassion for Christ. Compassion must be felt. Note, for example, the *Stabat Mater:* "Alas, O Mother, font of love, make me feel the strength of sorrow that I might mourn with you."

45 Cf. on *Mater misericordiae* F. J. E. Raby, *op. cit.,* pp. 450–51, and E. Mâle, *L'art religieux de la fin du moyen âge en France* (Paris 1908), pp. 205 ff.

46 L. Bréhier, *L'Art chrétien* (Paris 1928), pp. 288 ff.
47 *Ibid.*, pp. 391 ff.
48 R. H. Bainton, *Here I Stand* (New York 1950), p. 30.
49 L. W. Spitz, tr., *Luther's Works* 34 (Philadelphia 1960), pp. 26–27.
50 *The Good News Yesterday and Today*, p. 56.

of iniquity in the Church of God. Even a superficial reading of Church History is sufficient to uncover this dismal aspect of her character—apostasy from Christian faith and morals. To the uninstructed, to the naïve especially, the record of the pontificates of Sixtus IV (1471–84), Innocent VIII (1484–92) and Alexander VI (1492–1503) is enigmatic. It overwhelms with disedification, and invariably produces a *crise de foi* in the minds of those who have come to know the Church only as the kingdom of the perfect, the assembly of the stainless, the communion of saints. A disproportionate emphasis on infallibility in faith leads imperceptibly to a distorted concept of impeccability in morals. Neglected is the teaching of the Lord in the parables that the terrestrial Church is made up of both wheat and tares.

In the history of God's chosen people in the Old Testament the perfect prototype of the Church is discernible. Closely affiliated with the Lord in a solemn covenant and graciously called by Him from bondage, this chosen flock wandered in the wilderness towards the land of promise. They were not forsaken. For as God's beloved people they enjoyed His special guiding providence. By night He stood over them as a pillar of fire, by day as a cloud. With manna from heaven they were miraculously fed, and refreshed with water drawn in wondrous wise from a rock. A safe passage through the waters of the Red Sea secured them from Pharaoh and his threatening army. The divine assistance was real, sincere and constant. Yet the history of the Exodus shows that this God-led race, the chosen people, the object of the Lord's predilection, interrupted its peregrination to the terrestrial Jerusalem to adore a calf of gold, an act of supreme infidelity to the God who never for an instant deserted the people whom He had chosen.

These pages of Scripture are filled with insight and consolation for those who know how to read them. In the inconstancy of the chosen people of the old alliance is reflected the infidelity of the new chosen people, those of the Christian dispensation, the Church of Christ. As the former deviated en route to the terrestrial Jerusalem, so too the latter swerves from the path which leads to the celestial Jerusalem. In both Old and New Testaments the power of God is manifest, constant and victorious, for He is always with the people whom He calls His own. The book of Exodus shows God's people finally entering the land of promise under divine protection. Through the power of the same God His new people attain the promised heavenly Jerusalem, "the city of peace." Individuals apostasize and defect; but the whole Mystical Body, like the Body of Christ, moves forward to glory. In the last days it will rise and ascend to heaven, as its Head who has gone on before. Through the power of God it will enter into glory without end.

The history of the Church, therefore, is the history of God's people in the wilderness of this world. In ancient Christian terms this history, which is fundamentally prefigured in the Old Testament, begins with the death of Christ on the Cross; it coincides with the sixth age of the world, the last phase of world history. For God has done all and done all well. The "grace and truth" of Christ are at hand. It is an eschatological moment, the terminal era of redemption and salvation. The history of these last days, which is the record of Christ's continuing influence in this world, is compounded of many ingredients, of moments of exaltation and humiliation, of the sacred and the secular, of splendor and abjection. It is marked by individual fidelity and infidelity to the things of God, but absent is any trace of corporate deviation of the Church from her vocation to save men. For in her inner being she is inseparably united to Christ. Thus, in spite of the aberrations of this or that individual, or groups of individuals, the Church moves on through history under the protection of God to the splendid hour of the *eschata* when the Lord will come to take this beloved Spouse unto Himself.

In view of the high relevance of Church History to salvation history it is surprising, even disturbing, to note the very insignificant role that the history of the Church has played in Catholic intellectual life, especially in theological thought. It is as if an overpowering Neo-Platonism had seized upon theology and compelled it to focus on eternal, universal, abstract ideas, divorced from history and, therefore, from human life. In terms of this aprioristic, analytical and deductive approach to intellectual problems it is the abstract idea rather than the historical event that is central. Under the influence of late scholasticism a static theology, untouched by a vital sense of genetic development as a creative factor in human thought, was formed and became a legacy. Its method is characterized by a tendency to concentrate on the propositional rather than the historical; possibly to dislodge, at least to overlook or disregard history in favor of speculation.

That Catholic theology has been unhistorical in its intellectual comprehension of problems is a normal consequence of the historical past. In Christian antiquity there were Fathers of the Church, St. Athanasius (d. 373) and St. Augustine (d. 430) for example, who had an appreciation of the fact that the doctrinal issues of the day, Arianism and Pelagianism, had their roots in history, and that by laying bare these roots the character of the theological issues would be clarified. But medieval theology with its meager concern for historical reality was out of touch with this tradition. It is indicative that the medieval exegete adopted the mystical tradition of Alexandria rather than the historical tradition of Antioch. For example, in the exegetical method of Origen (d. *ca.* 254) the spiritual (allegorical, tropological and anagogic) sense of Scripture was valued as the heart of the sacred text. The literal (historical) sense was considered of minor importance, significant only to the simple, the unlettered and the adolescent. In consequence of this hermeneutics, history declined, while the mystical (theological) was exalted on the basis of Christian revelation: "The letter kills, but the spirit gives life."

The learned world of medieval theology in its preoccupation with the universal, the abstract and the essential had little interest in or sympathy with the singular, the concrete and the existential—the building blocks of history. It is of passing interest to note that the medieval anthropologist, while he felt himself capable of explaining the psychology of man's knowledge of universal essences, was somewhat at a loss to demonstrate how the isolated singular could be known. It is not by chance or oversight that Church History, or any other history save Biblical, did not enter into the curriculum of the medieval universities. And rare is the medieval theologian whose work gives evidence of a knowledge of history and historical method.

History was not traditionally part of the theologian's equipment. Dialectic was the master-key, especially in the late Middle Ages. The significance of the humanist movement of the circle of Erasmus (d. 1536), becomes clearer when it is understood as an attempt to bring Catholic theology back to its primitive sources, above all to Holy Scripture, the Fathers of the Church and ecclesiastical history. The spirit of this renaissance of Christian thought was a salutary antidote to the apriorism of the Schools. When one recalls that the humanist Cardinal Cervini had to remind the theologians at Trent of their obligation to read the Bible rather than to read about it, the character of late medieval theology becomes vivid. It becomes even more vivid when one studies the discussions at Trent which centered on the concept of tradition. The feeble attempts of the Fathers of the Council to discover the meaning and the content of tradition on the basis of their knowledge of Church History are evidence of the historical unawareness of the theologians of that day.

Abstract theological thought as the product of dialectic had well overreached itself by the first quarter of the sixteenth century. Luther among others sensed the disproportion, and on the basis of scholastic theology as he knew it, abnegated with a maximum of scorn and ridicule the old tradition in which he had been educated. The confessional polemic which the reformers of the sixteenth century launched posed serious historical problems which contemporary Catholic theologians were not in a position to handle. No amount of syllogistic reasoning could persuade Luther to forsake the facts of history (touching on the authority of councils and the supremacy of the papacy) as he knew them. Ultimately it was under the auspices of the reformers (Philip Melanchthon and Matthias Flacius) that historical method boldly confronted scholastic theology.

Even to this day Church History plays no significant role in seminary education which in many respects is a linear descendant of the medieval faculties of theology. Contemporary sacerdotal education finds an analogous archetype in medieval hermeneutics where the spiritual, not the literal (historical) sense of things is paramount. Theology (allegory), understood as scholastic theology, is 'queen of the sciences,' while moral (tropology) and ascetical (anagoge) theology are regarded as the practical disciplines of the pastoral life. Thus the priest, who is committed to a life-service of the Church, is far from enjoying a thorough acquaintance with her history. This means that his knowledge of the Church is one-sided in that it is more propositional and practical than historical and existential. He knows the Church dogmatically and legally; he understands her moral and ascetical teaching: but he does not know the Church as a living organism which has evolved through centuries of history.

Yet the priest who is to communicate the Church to the world must know her from all angles and under all aspects. This is suggested by the pointed words of Paul VI in *Ecclesiam suam* (August 6, 1964) when he writes:

The Church needs to reflect on herself. She needs to feel the throb of her own life. She must learn to know herself better, if she wishes to live her own proper vocation and to offer to the world her message of brotherhood and of salvation. She needs to experience Christ in herself.

Priestly education, therefore, should rest solidly on salvation history, that is, on biblical and ecclesiastical history whose central object is Christ, His Church and the "Mystical Body as it travels its pilgrim's way through time."

Parallel to the spirit of the older theologians who closed their eyes to history is another, more modern approach to theology which is inspired by the conviction that the science of theology begins—or should begin—with *now*. It is indifferent, if not hostile, to history. Past achievement is negated as *irrelevant* to the moment, as if the value of the past consists only in its inspirational appeal to the present. New paths, free from tradition, are sought; and the lessons of history are left unread. In its poetry the ideal of this conception of sacred doctrine as a theology of the present is noble; but the truth of the matter, if the testimony of history is reliable, lies in another direction— the same frustration that every past age has experienced in neglecting the living tradition of the Church's thought as it is discovered in history.

Without destroying youth, history confers on it the advantages of mature age, insight, wisdom, experience and judgment. It extends the power of man's vision far backward in time, to other cultural situations in which the Church has been involved in one way or another. This intellectual flexibility engenders a sense of evolution in which human thought, institutions and art, as well as spiritual and ascetical values, are seen to rise and fall. And in the midst of this ebb and flow which are characteristic of history, the divine and necessary elements of the Church come into focus beside the human and contingent. This sense of change and development is of high importance to the current epoch of the Church which under the name of *aggiornamento* has taken up the task of reformation. The task, if arduous, is also delicate, and requires the collaboration of specialists who know the Church as she was in order to be able to form her as she should be. To reform the Church means to make her over in accord with her pristine image. Paul VI in *Ecclesiam suam* states the problem of reform in these words:

. . . the term reform . . . is not to be understood in the sense of change, but of a stronger determination to preserve the characteristic features which Christ has impressed on the Church. We should rather always wish to lead her back to her perfect form corresponding, on the one hand, to her original design, and on the other, fully consistent with the necessary development which like a seed grown into a tree has given to the Church her legitimate and concrete form in history . . . We must serve the Church and love her as she is, with a clear understanding of history.

The appreciation of the point of view outlined in these few words must obviously rest on a knowledge and evaluation of Church History. Reform is not a matter of caprice or taste.

History opens up the past as generously as the extant sources allow. In presenting things as they once were, it should imitate justice in its impartiality, directness and courage. It may not respect persons. History can edify, but invariably it shatters. Before it, cherished traditions fall, heroes are brought down, catastrophes are rightfully, though painfully, traced to their responsible authors. Because history is candid, it almost always irritates; it seldom soothes. Its effect on the religious mind is often overwhelming. Thus, certain books are kept from young religious, because in them the holy founder is represented in a light different (though perhaps accurate) from the current tradition. Scandals (more often than not simple mistakes) are hidden lest this or that hero be seen in his true complexion as an ordinary human being, not a superman, but a simple child of God. To preserve reputation, especially of ecclesiastical superiors, archives have been destroyed with the fervent hope that unpleasant chapters of history might be obliterated. Historical investigation especially in the area of the history of spirituality has often been impeded lest it be discovered that certain revered traditions stem from sources of doubtful authenticity. Even the spiritual diary of a saint as distinguished as St. Therese of Lisieux (d. 1897) was altered to bring it into conformity with the preconceived ideas of her institute. History frightens indeed. But does it frighten so much that honesty and objectivity must be cast aside to preserve reputation, respectability and tradition?

There is about the primitive Christian community an openness in representing itself that is found wanting in the Church at other times and in other places. We are all well-acquainted with the bold, sure lines with which the Gospel traces out for all generations the repudiation of the Saviour by St. Peter and the unfortunate suicide of Judas, despondent after the betrayal of his Lord. The great Dominican orator Père Jean-Baptiste Lacordaire (d. 1861) addressed these words to Henri Perreyve, Oratorian and professor of Church History at the Sorbonne, on the question of objectivity in historical scholarship. They are worth repeating here:

Truth, when discreetly told, is an inestimable boon to mankind, and to suppress it, especially in history, is an act of cowardice unworthy of a Christian. Timidity is the fault of our age, and truth is concealed under pretense of respect for holy things. God indeed has conferred upon His Chuch the prerogative of infallibility, but to none of the members of His Church has He granted immunity from sin. Peter was a sinner and a renegade, and God has been at pains to have the fact recorded in the Gospels.

These words present a challenge to all ecclesiastical authority responsible for the scientific investigation and publication of Church History. That Church whose Head is "the way, the truth and the light" has in this matter a most special responsibility towards humanity.

If it be true that Christ taught men not only by what He said (words) but also by what He did (deeds), it is equally true that His Church teaches in this fashion. Both words and deeds are integral factors in salvation history; both, therefore, enter into the didactic purposes of the Church. The faithful learn by seeing and by hearing. Thus, those who studied the Passion-narrative of our Saviour and those who beheld the passion-event of St. Polycarp (d. *ca.* 155) were in truth instructed in the lesson of Christian witness. In dying, both Jesus and Polycarp were true witnesses (martyrs), the one to His Father, the other to his Lord. In the words of Holy Scripture the historical Christ lives on, in the pages of Church History the Mystical Christ is seen in action. By His abiding presence to His Church our Saviour acts in this world which He redeemed; and to study and to learn of the Christ acting in this world is to learn a profound lesson in Christian doctrine.

History is not an entertaining story without significance. It is a literary re-presentation of past reality, the affairs of man and God, interpreted in terms of the present. Through history as an open door we are allowed to enter the vast realm of the distant past, to inspect, explore and evaluate it. The darkness of *then* in a certain measure is illuminated in the full light of *now*. But at the same time we are illuminated by this intellectual experience, for history is in itself a liberal education for those who want to learn its lessons. It reveals, for example, how the catastrophes of yesterday might be avoided today, and it suggests ways and means of building a better future in terms of past experience. In this respect the pages of Church History are no exception. They are filled with lessons of contemporary significance which we may not easily overlook.

In the course of this book we have examined four Church problems, the ecclesial, biblical, liturgical and spiritual, which are rooted in Christian antiquity but which came to maturity in the late Middle Ages. To a large degree they formed the center of the target at which the Protestant polemic aimed its arrows. By the opening years of the sixteenth century these four problems, which were already inveterate, had crystallized. Ignored and disregarded over the years, these crystalline problems grew in size and solidity. The basic pattern remained the same. It is only in our own day, four hundred years after the close of the Council of Trent (1563), that the current ecumenical council is giving them proper consideration, for the questions which they pose touch the very heart and fiber of the Church and her mission in this world.

One of the most pressing current ecclesiological problems is collegiality, which raises the question of the feasibility of allotting to the episcopacy as a group (college of bishops) a more significant and responsible role in the administrative structure of the universal Church. Collegiality as such is not an innovation. For at present the Church is administered by a *collegium*, the college of cardinals, who according to canon law (c. 230) form the senate of the Roman Pontiff. In an earlier chapter we have seen how this college was born, grew and developed into an aristocratic oligarchy that almost overwhelmed both Church and papacy. Throughout the last five hundred years there has always been a certain tension between curial cardinals and the ordinary bishops of the Church. The contemporary problem of collegiality far from being new has its foundations in the past.

More than five centuries ago, at the Council of Constance (1414–18), important voices were sharply raised against the cardinals and all they represented; and a thorough reform of the Roman *Curia* was demanded in terms that left no doubt that its external prestige had fallen low. In its saner moments the Council of Basle (1431–39) made moves to submit the curial cardinals to a vigorous reformation. A century later Paul III (1534–49) was informed by his reform commission that all the ecclesiastical evils (and they were enormous) were traceable to the Roman *Curia* itself. And despite the measures that that intrepid pope took in view of the fact that the Church lay in ruins, the *status quo* of this élite was preserved. The hope of curial reform has never been totally absent from the Church during the past centuries since the late Middle Ages. Yet the Roman *Curia* has retained successfully its authority and its centrality in the Church. Does it seem likely that a curial reformation of any imposing dimensions will take place in our day? Hardly. For an institution that has been able to maintain itself over more than nine hundred years in the face of every grave crisis and furious onslaught is not apt to vanish easily from the stage of history.

In handling the problems of Bible and liturgy the Second Vatican Council has done a noble service for the Church. In a solemn manner it has reorientated the faithful to these two fonts of Catholic life in a way that will inevitably, if faithfully prosecuted, terminate in a spiritual renaissance. Two statements from the *Constitution on the Sacred Liturgy* illustrate the tenor of the Council's thought in these matters:

The liturgy is the summit towards which the activity of the Church is directed. At the same time it is the fount from which all her power flows. For the aim and object of apostolic works is that all who are made sons of God by faith and baptism should come together to praise God in the midst of His Church, to take part in the sacrifice and to eat the Lord's Supper.

And the *Constitution* urges communal worship, built on Christian faith and charity; it allows generous use of the vernacular, inculcates liturgical education, urges simplicity of rite and language. The whole teaching of the *Constitution* is inspired by a deep concern for the cultivation of Christian piety in terms of sound theological doctrine. One may well wonder what path the history of the Church would have followed had the Council of Trent promulgated this *Constitution* four hundred years ago. And one may well wonder what path the history of the Church will follow if this *Constitution* is neglected by those Catholic pastors to whom the care of souls is committed.

Even a superficial reading of this document shows a marked transition in the Church's approach to Holy Scripture. The Bible takes on here an authentic mystical quality. No longer a book of religious stories, a source book of proofs, a mirror of moral perfection, an esoteric book in an unknown sacred tongue, the Bible is now described as the record of salvation, God's Word spoken to man. But even more than that, Scripture occupies a high place in the sanctification of the Christian. For here in the New Testament one hears Christ Himself once again proclaiming His saving Gospel to all men. "He is present in His word, since it is He Himself who speaks when the Holy Scriptures are read in the Church." Accordingly the Council prescribes that,

The treasures of the Bible are to be opened up more lavishly, so that richer fare may be provided for the faithful at the table of God's Word.

The whole tenor of the conciliar teaching is to produce a more biblical minded Church. In the decades ahead the effect will be most remarkable in Catholic spiritual life, which under the inspiration of Word and Sacrament will know a new freedom from outmoded prayer forms and devotions, a new freedom to turn more directly and uniquely to Christ the Lord as the center of all Catholic life.

In our own day we are witnessing the solution of the great problems of centuries ago. The Church is being reformed by that Spirit who in a peculiar way enlightens the hearts of the faithful. We have called upon Him with sincerity and humility; and now that His generous assistance is with us we must have the courage to work to the end. But the *reformed* Church will always remain a Church *to be reformed*. Because though divine in her soul, she is always human in her members. Reformation is an arduous task; it breaks hearts as the old, the cherished, the traditional flow away. Paul VI has described the character of our task in these words:

The actual image of the Church is never as perfect, as lovely, as holy or as brilliant as that formative divine idea would wish it to be. Hence there arises the unselfish and almost impatient need for renewal, for correction of the defects which this conscience denounces and rejects, as if, standing before a mirror, we were to examine interiorly the image of Christ which He has left us.

The consoling element in this vast work is the lofty purpose at which it aims—the rediscovery of Christ in His Church and the proclamation of Him as Priest, Mediator and Head to the world which He redeemed and saves.

Chronology

800	Imperial coronation of Charles the Great.
804	Alcuin dies.
962–1002	The Ottonian Emperors.
1046	Synod of Sutri.
1054	Schism between the Latin and Greek Churches.
1059	Reform decree of Nicholas II on papal elections.
1072	St. Peter Damiani dies.
1076	Excommunication of Henry IV by Gregory VII.
1077	Henry IV does penance at Canossa.
1085	Gregory VII dies at Salerno.
1096–1099	First Crusade.
1122	Concordat at Worms: Callixtus II and Henry V.
1123	First Lateran Council.
1139	Second Lateran Council.
1153	St. Bernard dies.
1179	Third Lateran Council.
1198	Innocent III is elected pope.
1215	Fourth Lateran Council.
1226	St. Francis of Assisi dies.
1245	First Council of Lyons.
1274	St. Thomas Aquinas dies.
	Second Council of Lyons.
	St. Bonaventure dies.
1296	*Clericis laicos* of Boniface VIII.
1302	*Unam sanctam* of Boniface VIII.
1303	The 'affairs' of Anagni.
1309–1377	The Avignon papacy.
1316–1334	John XXII.
1339–1453	Hundred Years War (England vs. France).
1348–1350	Black Death.
1378–1417	Great Western Schism.

1384	The Lollard Bible: Wycliffe's circle.
1409	Council of Pisa.
1414–1418	Council of Constance.
1415	John Huss is executed in Constance.
	Sacrosancta (sess. 5: Council of Constance).
1417	Martin V is elected pope. Great Western Schism ends.
1431	St. Joan of Arc is executed in Rouen.
1431–1449	Council of Basle.
1438–1445	Council of Florence.
1447–1534	Renaissance popes.
1450–1455	Gutenberg's Bibles appear in Mainz.
1451	Felix V, the last anti-pope, dies.
1492–1503	Alexander VI.
1498	Savonarola is executed in Florence.
1512–1517	Fifth Lateran Council.
1514	*Complutum* of Cardinal Ximénes is printed.
1516	Erasmus' New Testament in Greek.
1517	Luther's Ninety-Five Theses.
1521	Diet of Worms.
1522	Luther's New Testament in German.
	Complutum appears.
1525	Tyndale's Bible in English.
	Luther's German Mass.
1528	Mathias Grünewald dies.
1530	Confession of Augsburg.
1530	Thomas More's *Dialogue Concerning Tyndale*.
1534–1549	Paul III.
1535	Cardinal Quiñones' *Breviary of the Holy Cross*.
	Institutes of John Calvin.
1537	*Consilium de emendanda ecclesia*.
1545–1563	Council of Trent.

1546   Luther dies.

1548   *Spiritual Exercises* of St. Ignatius Loyola.

1553   Michael Servetus is executed in Geneva.

1564   John Calvin dies.

1568   Roman Breviary of St. Pius V is published.

1570   Roman Missal of St. Pius V is published.

1582   Douai-Reims Bible in English.

1588   Sacred Congregation of Rites is established.

1648   Treaty of Westphalia.

1655–1667 Alexander VII.

1869–1870 First Vatican Council.

1905   St. Pius X: Decree on daily Communion.

1943   Pius XII: *Mystici Corporis.*

       Pius XII: *Divino Afflante Spiritu.*

1947   Pius XII: *Mediator Dei.*

1962   Second Vatican Council opens.

1963   Vatican Constitution on the Sacred Liturgy.

1964   Vatican Constitution on the Church.

Bibliography

K. Adam, *The Roots of the Reformation* (New York 1951).

L. Bouyer, *Liturgical Piety* (Notre Dame 1955).

Y. M. J. Congar, *Lay People in the Church* (Westminster 1957).

M. Deanesly, *The Lollard Bible* (Cambridge 1920).

P. Hughes, *A History of the Church* 3 (New York 1947).

J. Huizinga, *The Waning of the Middle Ages* (New York 1954).

E. F. Jacob, *Essays in the Conciliar Epoch* (Notre Dame 1963).

H. Jedin, *A History of the Council of Trent* 1 (St. Louis 1957).

H. Jedin, *Ecumenical Councils of the Catholic Church* (New York 1960).

J. Jungmann, *Pastoral Liturgy* (New York 1962).

J. Jungmann, *The Early Liturgy* (Notre Dame 1962).

J. Jungmann, *The Good News Yesterday and Today* (New York 1962).

H. Küng, *Structures of the Church* (New York 1963).

J. Lortz, *How the Reformation Came* (New York 1964).

J. Lortz, *The Reformation* (Westminster 1964).

R. McNally, *The Reform of the Church* (New York 1963).

R. McNally, *The Bible in the Early Middle Ages,* Woodstock Papers 4 (Westminster 1959).

A. Mirgeler, *Mutations of Western Christianity* (New York 1964).

G. Mollat, *The Popes at Avignon 1305–78* (New York 1963).

H. Oberman, *The Harvest of Medieval Theology* (Cambridge, Mass. 1963).

W. Schwarz, *Principles and Problems of Biblical Translation* (Cambridge 1955).

B. Smalley, *The Study of the Bible in the Middle Ages* (Oxford 1952).

L. Spitz, *The Religious Renaissance of the German Humanists* (Cambridge, Mass. 1963).

B. Tierney, *Foundations of the Conciliar Theory* (Cambridge 1963).

W. Ullmann, *The Origins of the Great Schism* (London 1948).

T. Westow, *The Variety of Catholic Attitudes* (New York 1963).

Index *